S.S.

GREAT BRITAIN

S.S. Great Britain represents one of the most significant stages in the transition from sail to mechanically driven ships. She was as important in her time to marine engineering as the first jet-driven passenger aircraft, the De Havilland Comet, was to aeronautical development some hundred years later.

It may all look so easy and almost primitive in our eyes today but when she was built she included more 'firsts' than any ship since man first learnt to sail over the oceans.

Men have always made a distinction between great works of art and works of convenience but it seems to me that we should recognise works of genius in whatever form they may appear. Lovely buildings and architectural masterpieces are not the only structures which deserve our admiration and therefore preservation. The "Great Britain" was the creation of a man of genius, an imaginative and original engineer at a time when the whole potential of technology lay before those who could grasp its opportunities. Brunel ranks with that relatively small group of people who have made a decisive impact on the course of human history.

The hull of his great ship is still intact and enough detail is known of her fittings and equipment for her to be restored to her original condition. This surely should be done because she will always be unique and she will always remain a thing of wonder and fascination for generations into the future.

S.S. GREAT BRITAIN

Adrian Ball
&
Diana Wright

DAVID & CHARLES

NEWTON ABBOT   LONDON   NORTH POMFRET (VT)

Library of Congress Catalog Card Number 80-68903

Typeset by ABM Typographics, Hull
Printed in Great Britain
by Ebenezer Baylis & Son Ltd., The Trinity Press,
Worcester, and London
for David & Charles (Publishers) Limited
Brunel House Newton Abbot Devon

Published in the United States of America
by David & Charles Inc
North Pomfret Vermont 05053 USA

British Library Cataloguing in Publication Data

Ball, Adrian
    S.S. Great Britain
    I. Title II. Wright, Diana
    623.8′243   VM383.G6

ISBN 0-7153-8096-6

ACKNOWLEDGEMENTS

The authors wish to express their deep gratitude to Dr Ewan Corlett, the distinguished naval architect, whose enthusiastic interest in the SS *Great Britain* sparked the campaign to save her in 1968. Dr Corlett has amassed a unique collection of material on the vessel and he gave the authors unrestricted access to it. Many illustrations in these pages come from the archives he has assembled with great skill and devotion over half a lifetime.

The delightful line and water colour reconstructions of the steamship as she was in 1845 are the work of students at the Bournemouth & Poole College of Art. The names of the talented young artists responsible are Ian Carter (page 6), Lionel Jeans (page 12), David Ditcher and Joan-Marie Abley (page 16), Timothy Davies (page 20, upper), Phillip Cox (page 20, lower) and Stephen Palfrey (page 21). Thanks are due to Michael E. Leek and to Stanley Paine of the College's School of Technical Illustration, who directed the preparation of the illustrations and gave support during the preparation of this volume.

Invaluable advice came, too, from Commander Joe Blake of the SS *Great Britain* Project, and his colleagues at the Great Western Dock. As the Project Director, Cdr Blake has been involved in the reconstruction work on the vessel since her early days in Bristol. Under his supervision the dock museum has grown steadily in its scope and the number of exhibits.

There is insufficient space to acknowledge the debt of marine enthusiasts to the many people who have saved relics of the SS *Great Britain* for generations and have then turned them over to the Project's care. The authors trust that the generosity of such men and women will be partly rewarded by seeing their family mementoes illustrated in this book. Finally, numerous artists and photographers are responsible for the large number of illustrations displayed herein and their names are normally credited in the narrative, at appropriate points.

The perspective cutaway of the 1845 vessel, shown on the jacket, with all interior fittings, engines and boilers removed to reveal the basic structure, was drawn by Lionel Jeans.

INTRODUCTION

The date was late 1835, the place Radleys Hotel in Blackfriars, a stone's throw from London's bustling Fleet Street. A meeting was taking place of directors of the Great Western Railway Company. In attendance was Isambard Kingdom Brunel, consulting engineer to the fast-growing railway enterprise. Brunel, son of the distinguished engineer Sir Marc Brunel, was only in his thirtieth year but was already showing the flair and the boldness which was to win him the reputation of being the outstanding engineer of the nineteenth century.

The discussion turned to the length of the GWR line from Paddington to Bristol (120 miles) and Brunel remarked suddenly that the line could be made longer by extending it to New York. All that was required was to build a steamship, perhaps called the *Great Western*, which could sail regularly between Bristol and the thriving American city. A passenger wishing to cross the Atlantic could then go to Paddington and buy a through ticket to New York.

It was typical of Brunel that he should make so revolutionary a proposal to his seniors, and equally typical of the energetic GWR directors that they should take him seriously. A three-man committee was appointed at once to examine the idea in detail. It was a scheme as breath-taking for its time as was the concept of crossing the Atlantic at supersonic speeds in Concorde.

In January of 1836 the committee submitted an encouraging report to the GWR board and it was resolved to form the Great Western Steamship Company to build the ship. Brunel had urged on the committee the economic advantages of large vessels and they duly recommended that the ship should be of at least 1,200 tons. Such a steamer, they felt, would be able to travel to New York from Bristol in less than 20 days and return in 13. In those days the average sailing ship took 36 days out and 24 home.

So the building of the *Great Western*, a wooden ship powered by paddles, began that year in Bristol. She was launched on 19 July 1837 and commenced her 15-day maiden voyage on 8 April 1838. She came home in 14 days and the first Atlantic ferry service had begun. Although the ship narrowly missed the honour of being the first to cross the Atlantic under steam, she was, as her owners claimed, the first vessel 'laid down, equipped and sent to sea for the purpose of establishing a steam line between America and England'.

The immediate commercial success of the *Great Western* encouraged her owners to build a consort and in September 1838 they announced plans for a wooden vessel of the same size to be known as the *City of New York*. But soon, under Brunel's influence, the project changed to something far more imaginative. During that year and the next, five versions of the new vessel were planned, each larger than its predecessor, with iron finally replacing wood for the hull. And, as the concept grew in daring, the name was changed to *Mammoth*, considered to be more appropriate for a ship which would be twice as large as anything afloat.

In 1840 Brunel turned the project upside down with a masterly report that urged the scrapping of the side paddles and the adoption of screw propulsion, then in its infancy. That report followed a close study over several months of an experimental vessel called the *Archimedes*, built to demonstrate the feasibility of propeller-driven craft. Brunel became convinced that the successor to the *Great Western* must have the new form of drive, largely unproven though it was. He told the board his opinion was 'strong and decidedly in favour of the advantage of employing the screw in the new ship'. But he added he was fully aware of the responsibilities he was taking upon himself in giving that advice.

So the order for the original engines was scrapped and Brunel began the search for new machinery to drive a propeller mighty enough to take a leviathan across the Atlantic. Although work on the iron ship had started in the last weeks of 1839, it was not until the spring of 1841 that the revised construction programme really got under way. By then she was named the *Great Britain*, the first vessel to embody all the elements of the modern ship, with her metal construction, steam power, screw propulsion, and large size. The *Great Britain* has a proud and permanent place in marine history—and, happily, is still with us, thanks to a rescue operation bold enough to have been conceived by Brunel himself . . .

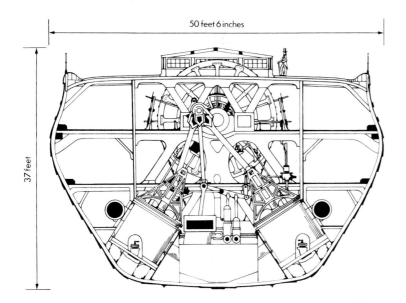

A modern artist's reconstruction of Brunel's 1845 1,000hp, 18 revolutions-per-minute engine which powered the original *Great Britain*. It was built in the workshops of the Great Western Steamship Company under the direction of Thomas Guppy, but Brunel played a large part in the design of this remarkable machinery. Much of the inspiration came from Sir Marc Brunel's 1822 invention of the 'Triangle' engine—the first 'vee' engine—which drove upwards to a crankshaft above the cylinders.

When the decision was taken to give the *Great Britain* screw propulsion, Brunel took the bold step of positioning the engines across the ship so that they could drive the propeller shaft. At the time of the ship's maiden voyage this power unit was undoubtedly the most unusual and advanced steam engine in the world. A contemporary model of the original machinery (*right*) has been preserved in London's Science Museum. With the help of engineering concerns all over Britain, a full-size replica was under construction, for ultimate positioning in the ship at Bristol, as this book was being written.

Guppy set down his plans for construction of the hull of the *Great Britain* in a description of his invention, most of which is reproduced on the opposite page. Thomas Guppy, a Bristol merchant and engineer, was one of the original committee deputed by the GWR board to consider the practicality of building an Atlantic steamship. The others were Captain Christopher Claxton, a retired naval officer, and William Patterson, a Bristol shipbuilder. All three men were involved in the great adventure which began with the *Great Western* paddle steamer and led to the construction of the *Great Britain*.

A.D. 1843 . . . . Nº 9779.

Building Metal Ships, &c.

GUPPY'S SPECIFICATION.

TO ALL TO WHOM THESE PRESENTS SHALL COME, I, THOMAS RICHARD GUPPY, of the Great Western Iron Ship Building and Steam Engine Works, Bristol, send greeting.

WHEREAS Her present most Excellent Majesty Queen Victoria, by Her
5 Letters Patent under the Great Seal of Great Britain, bearing date at Westminster, the Fifteenth day of June, in the sixth year of Her reign, did, for Herself, Her heirs and successors, give and grant unto me, the said Thomas Richard Guppy, Her especial licence, full power, sole privilege and authority, that I, the said Thomas Richard Guppy, my exõrs, admõrs, and
10 assigns, or such others as I, the said Thomas Richard Guppy, my exõrs, admõrs, or assigns, should at any time agree with, and no others, from time to time and at all times during the term of years therein expressed, should and lawfully might make, use, exercise, and vend, within England, Wales, and the Town of Berwick-upon-Tweed, my Invention of "CERTAIN IMPROVEMENTS
15 IN THE BUILDING OF METAL SHIPS AND OTHER VESSELS;" in which said Letters Patent is contained a proviso that I, the said Thomas Richard Guppy, shall cause a particular description of the nature of my said Invention, and in what manner the same is to be performed, to be inrolled in Her said Majesty's High Court of Chancery within six calendar months next and
20 immediately after the date of the said in part recited Letters Patent, as in and by the same, reference being thereunto had, will more fully and at large appear.

Price 4s 6d

NOW KNOW YE, that in compliance with the said proviso, I, the said Thomas Richard Guppy, do hereby declare the nature of my said Invention to consist,—

First, in the substitution of plates of copper, or other suitable alloys of metal, instead of plates of iron, for such exterior parts of the bottoms and sides of 5 ships or vessels as are exposed to or are liable to be acted on by the water surrounding them.

Secondly, in the casing over, or what is commonly called sheathing, the bottoms of iron ships or vessels with copper or other suitable alloys of metal.

Thirdly, in the construction of false internal sides and bottoms to metal ships 10 or vessels, such false sides and bottoms being made of sheet iron or other metal, and placed at a suitable distance from the external bottoms and sides, and the space between being divided into compartments or spaces, as shewn in Figure 1, 2, 3, and 4.

Fourthly, in the application of metal hollow air-tight thwarts and seats to 15 metal boats.

And in further compliance with the said proviso, I, the said Thomas Richard Guppy, do hereby describe the manner in which my said Invention is to be performed, by the following statement thereof, reference being had to the Drawing annexed, and to the figures marked thereon (that is to say):— 20

First, as regards the substitution of other metals for iron plates, it is only necessary to state, that they are to be put together in the same manner as ordinary iron plates, the rivets being of metal similar to the plates.

Secondly, as regards the sheathing of iron ships or vessels, it is only necessary to state, that instead of nails rivets must be used, and the sheathing 25 and plates of the bottoms and sides properly drilled or pierced to receive the same.

Thirdly, as regards the construction of the false bottoms and sides to metal ships or vessels, and of the compartments or spaces between, the ordinary mode of using angle or T iron or other metal may be adopted, which will be easily 30 understood by any competent workman by referring to Figures 1, 2, 3, and 4, in the Drawing annexed.

Fourthly, as regards air-tight thwarts and seats for boats, Figures 5 and 6 shew an air-tight thwart; *a* being the side of the boat, *b* the top side of the thwart, *c* the under side of the thwart, *d* the angle iron connecting it to the boat. 35 Figures 7 and 8 shew a seat on my plan rivetted, also air-tight.

Now whereas I claim as my Invention the improvements herein-before described; and such my Invention being, to the best of my knowledge and belief, entirely new, and never before used within that part of Her said Majesty's

BANQUET
ON OCCASION OF
HIS ROYAL HIGHNESS PRINCE ALBERT'S
NAMING THE GREAT BRITAIN,
ON THE 19TH OF JULY, 1843.

BILL OF FARE for Table D, Section 3.

	Lamb.	
Jelly.		Noyeau Cream.
	Ornamented Savoy Cake.	
Fruit.		Fruit.
	Roast Fowls.*	
Chicken à la Báchamel.		Lobster Sallad.
	Perugat Pie.	
Charlot à la Russe.		Tourte and Coronet.
	Pièce Montée.	
Eels in Aspic.		Meriton of Ham.
	Basket of Prawns.	
Fruit.		Fruit.
	Tongue.*	
Petite d'Amour.		Jelly.
	Caramil Basket.	
Meriton of Ham.		Dressed Crabs.
	Bridge of Pastry.	
Italian Cream.		Almond Pastry.
	Roast Chicken.	
Fruit.		Fruit.
	CENTRE ORNAMENT.	
Lobster Sallad.		Poulet Farce.
	Saddle of Lamb.	
Almond Pudding.		Charlot à la Russe.
	Built Pastry.	
Fruit.		Fruit.
	Chantilly.	
Savoury Meriton.		Lobster in Aspic.
	Tongue.*	
Jelly.		Fancy Pastry.
	Basket of Prawns.	
Fruit.		Fruit.
	Pièce Montée.	
Italian Sallad.		Ham in Meriton.
	Raised Pie.	
Faunchenettes.		Meringue Pyramid.
	Roast Fowls.*	
Fruit.		Fruit.
	Almond Savoy Cake.	
Italian Cream.		Jelly.
	Roulard de Veau.	

* To be Removed by ICES. Strawberry, Cream. Lemon, Water. Vanilla, Cream. Currant, Water.

DRINKABLES Champagne. Port Sherry Light Wines. Iced Punch. Ditto Lemonade.

R. HAZARD, Contractor.

PHILP AND EVANS, PRINTERS, BRISTOL.

CARD OF ADMISSION
TO THE
Great Western Steam Ship Comp.'s Yard
TO VIEW THE LAUNCH OF
THE GREAT BRITAIN,
ON WEDNESDAY, JULY 19TH, 1843.

The expenses occasioned for the gratification of the Public being necessarily great, the price of this Ticket is 5s.

The Gates will not be opened before Half-past 11, and the Launch will take place at about 3. The entrance will be by the Cumberland Road only, and not by the way of the Towing Path.

⁎ Banquet Tickets are One Guinea each.

The date for the launching was set as 19 July 1843: an auspicious day for the Great Western Steamship Company as work on the vessel had begun four years earlier to the day; and 19 July also marked the sixth anniversary of the launch of the *Great Western*. Guests paid five shillings for tickets to view the event at the dock (*above*) and a further one guinea to enjoy a sumptuous cold banquet (*left*).

Prince Albert was guest of honour in a royal pavilion erected for the day by the entrance to the dock. He travelled to and from Bristol by the Great Western Railway, and marvelled at the fact that each train journey took only 2 hours 40 minutes. Queen Victoria's consort was invited to launch the vessel with a bottle of Champagne but he surrendered the honour to Mrs John Miles, wife of a Great Western director. Her aim, however, was at fault and she missed the ship. Prince Albert saved the day by seizing a second bottle and scoring a direct hit as the *Great Britain* was pulled slowly out of the dock. The time was 3.15 pm and that moment was recorded by a contemporary painting (*opposite top*). The lower painting captured the scene ten minutes later.

The Great Western Steamship Company's 600 distinguished guests who packed the elegant white and crimson royal pavilion, were joined in their celebrations by tens of thousands of Bristolians who decked the city with flags and bunting and crowded every vantage point around the dock. The floating harbour swarmed with small boats and barges of every description. A local newspaper estimated that 50,000 people had a commanding view of the event from Brandon Hill. Bristol, in fact, was not to have so exciting a marine occasion until 19 July 1970 when the *Great Britain* came home.

The royalist fervour which greeted Prince Albert was echoed in the design of the new steamship, the prow of which was dominated by a splendid gilt version of the royal arms, 6ft high and flanked by a lion to starboard and a unicorn to port. Running back from the figure-head were white trailboards, 16ft long, which depicted symbols of Victorian learning, art, trade, industry and agriculture. On the port side (*below left*) were displayed a coil of rope, gear wheels, a dove of peace, a carpenter's square, and a caduceus (the symbol of Mercury). To starboard (not illustrated) the symbols were a sheaf of corn, a globe, a lyre and trumpets, an artist's pallet, a book and a bunch of flowers.

INTERIOR OF "THE GREAT BRITAIN" STEAM-SHIP.

This stupendous steam-ship has been inspected by crowds of visitors during the past week. She continues moored off Blackwall, close to the terminus of the Railway, of which economical access thousands have availed themselves.

Although we have already illustrated the construction of this "interesting monster" (see Nos. 63 and 138 of our Journal), there remain to be described her interior fittings. Their style partakes of that plainness and simplicity which characterizes the entire vessel. In this respect consists her claim to

admiration, as well as in the vastness of her proportions, and the rigid utilitarianism with which not one inch of space is thrown away. In illustration of the latter, we annex two engravings, in which the situation of the machinery, and the general interior accommodation, are clearly seen at one view.

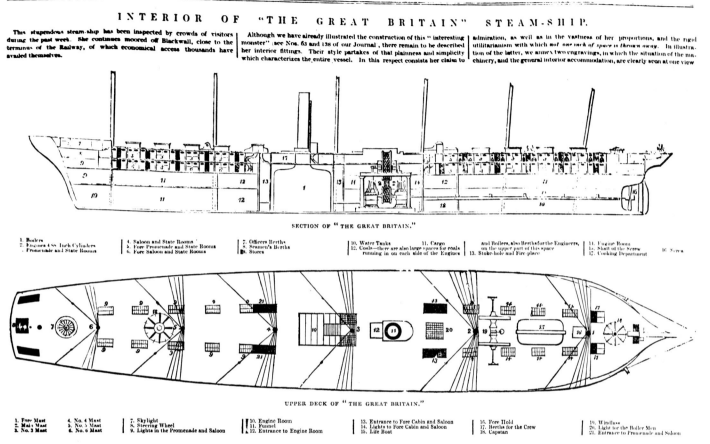

SECTION OF "THE GREAT BRITAIN."

1. Boilers
2. Engines 4 88 Inch Cylinders
3. Promenade and State Rooms
4. Saloon and State Rooms
5. Fore Promenade and State Rooms
6. Fore Saloon and State Rooms
7. Officers Berths
8. Seamen's Berths
9. Stores
10. Water Tanks
11. Cargo
12. Coals—there are also large spaces for coals running in on each side of the Engines

and Boilers, also Berths for the Engineers, on the upper part of this space
13. Stoke-hole and Fire-place
14. Engine Room
15. Shaft of the Screw
16. Screw
17. Cooking Department

UPPER DECK OF "THE GREAT BRITAIN."

1. Fore Mast
2. Main Mast
3. No. 3 Mast
4. No. 4 Mast
5. No. 5 Mast
6. No. 6 Mast
7. Skylight
8. Steering Wheel
9. Lights in the Promenade and Saloon
10. Engine Room
11. Funnel
12. Entrance to Engine Room
13. Entrance to Fore Cabin and Saloon
14. Lights to Fore Cabin and Saloon
15. Life Boat
16. Fore Hold
17. Berths for the Crew
18. Capstan
19. Windlass
20. Light for the Boiler Men
21. Entrance to Promenade and Saloon

The *Great Britain*'s dimensions were exceptional: her displacement was an unprecedented 3,675 tons, her length 322ft overall, and her breadth 50ft 6in. Her original registration certificate (*left*) was dated 10 January 1845 and gave the vessel the number 25967 which she has kept throughout her existence.

Her registered owners were stated to be 'John William Miles and Thomas Bonville Were of the City of Bristol, Trustees of the joint stock company called the Great Western Steamship Company'. The vessel was described quaintly as a 'schooner rigged with standing bowsprit, square stern and carvel built with false galleries and a royal arms figurehead'. As can be seen, this certificate was cancelled in 1852 when the ship was refitted.

While the directors were registering the new pride and joy of their company, an anonymous *Illustrated London News* artist was recording for posterity the plan and the interior of the vessel. The same artist made the sketches of the saloon and promenade decks which are reproduced on page 18. But for the journalistic and artistic enterprise of that publication, we would have little idea of the life-style devised for the passengers. The journal praised the 'plainness and simplicity' of the interior fittings and commented: 'In this respect consists her claim to admiration, as well as in the vastness of her proportions, and the rigid utilitarianism with which not one inch of space is thrown away.'

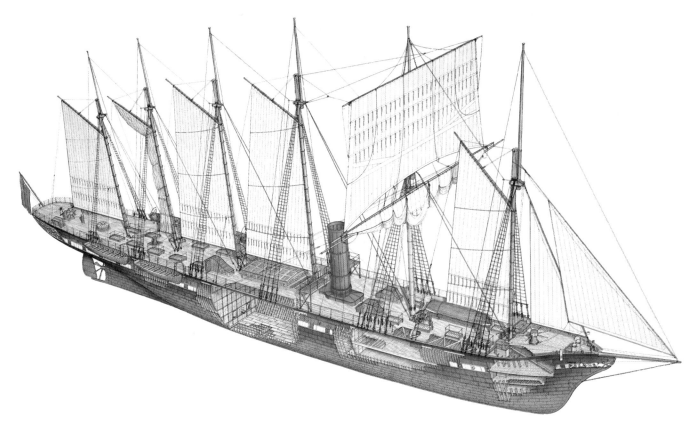

More than a century and a quarter after the *Illustrated London News* artist had put down his pen, young enthusiasts at the Bournemouth and Poole College of Art were engaged in a series of loving reconstructions of the ship which decorate these pages. The line and wash drawing (*above*) is a perspective view showing the hull cut away with all interior fittings removed to reveal the basic structure. She is shown with most of her sails set, those omitted being the gaff topsails on the fore and aft masts and the flying jib. The *Great Britain* was designed to carry 16,000sq ft of sail, a vast expanse but far less than would have been required for a sailing ship of similar size. In this illustration, the engines and boilers have been removed to give some idea of the double bottom and the bulkheads.

The *Great Britain* spent the period from July 1843 until January 1845 fitting out in Bristol and preparing for her sea trials. This was an anxious period for her owners as costs were mounting with each month that passed. In December 1843 they voted a further £10,000 to the project, carrying the expected total outlay beyond the £100,000 mark, against the £76,000 originally envisaged.

The final official cost of the vessel was recorded by the Great Western Steamship Company with Victorian precision as £117,295 6s 7d. That did not include the outlay on the shipyard which remained a separate asset. Of the total amount spent on the ship, 73 per cent went into making the hull and machinery, 15 per cent was devoted to the fittings, rigging and stores, while the balance represented financial charges and other items. The *Great Britain* cost roughly double that of the *Great Western* which was, of course, a much smaller and less complex vessel. Even in early Victorian days there was a small element of inflation.

One reason for the slow fitting out of the *Great Britain* during 1844 was her very size. She was, in fact, almost too large for Bristol's inner harbour system, devised in the early years of the nineteenth century. To reach the sea, the *Great Britain* had to negotiate the floating harbour and then pass through locks into the Cumberland Basin. From the basin there was another lock to enter the River Avon which itself had a horse-shoe bend limiting the length of vessels able to use the river (*right*).

Bristol's Dock Board was reluctant to widen the locks and the Board of Trade had to bring pressure to bear on the cautious and unimaginative local worthies. During this anxious period, the *Mechanics Magazine* described the ship as being 'in the predicament of a fattened weasel that, while feeding and fattening in the farmer's granary, grew too big for the hole by which it gained admission'. Work on widening the lock finally got under way in the autumn of 1844, and by December the *Great Britain* was ready to enter the Avon.

An attempt was made on the 10th of that month, but the vessel stuck passing through the lock. Further demolition of the masonry was necessary, under Brunel's supervision, and she did not float through into the river until the morning of the 12th. The painting (*above*) captures the exciting moment when the ship was free in the Avon and about to depart for her sea trials.

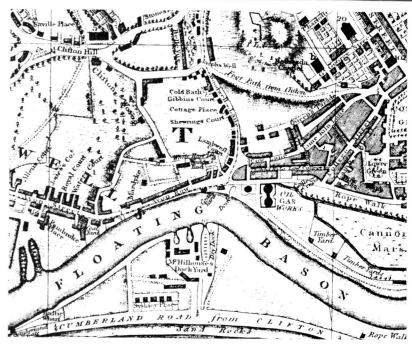

In addition to all her other 'firsts', the *Great Britain* was almost certainly the first ship to be photographed. The man behind the camera was William Henry Fox Talbot, who developed the process of photography known as 'Talbotypes' during the late 1830s and early 1840s. As early as 1834 Fox Talbot had been producing fixed camera images on paper—the very first negatives. He lived at Lacock Abbey, near Bath, so many of his early subjects were West Country scenes.

In April of 1844, while the iron ship was being fitted out in Cumberland Basin, Fox Talbot took the study above. At that time, the vessel was nearing completion and her machinery had been installed. The survival of certain buildings included in the Fox Talbot photograph makes it possible to identify the landing stage as the Northern Gas Ferry Steps.

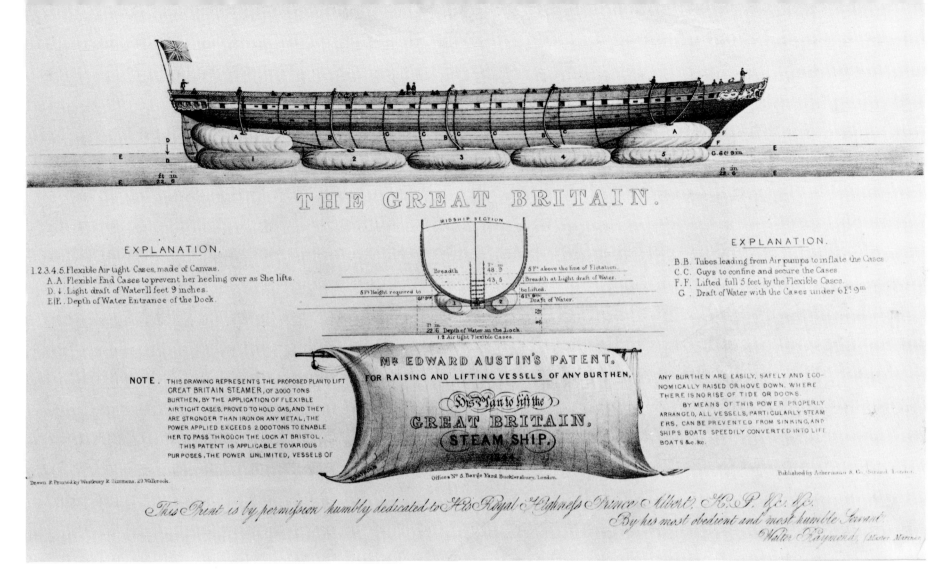

The plight of the *Great Britain*, possibly condemned to be imprisoned within the confines of Bristol's floating harbour, sent one Edward Austin to the drawing board in 1844. Here is the ingenious scheme he devised for floating the ship above the narrow locks by means of inflatable gas bags, capable, he calculated, of lifting the vast vessel. He went on to patent this scheme for 'raising and lifting vessels of any burthen'.

The confident Mr Austin declared in his application that 'by means of this power properly arranged all vessels, particularly steamers, can be prevented from sinking and ships' boats speedily converted into life boats etc etc'. The safe, if breath-taking, passage of the Brunel ship into the Avon in December 1844 must have sent Mr Austin in search of other potential clients.

15

Public interest in Brunel's latest masterpiece had been subdued during most of 1844 amid reports of financial problems and difficulties in getting her out of harbour. But once the ship was floating freely in the Avon in mid-December, the excitement began to mount, fanned by an admiring press. As she set off on brief steering trials a Liverpool newspaper reported: 'The contours presented to the eye are of the most exquisite grace—fine and beautifully rounded in her lines with a gentle sheer she sits upon the water like a racing gig.'

At sea for the first time, the engines functioned perfectly and Guppy sanctioned a speed of 11 knots. A correspondent of *The Times* aboard reported that the engines worked 'without the slightest vibration or tremor being felt in any part of the vessel'. A delighted Guppy went home to report to his directors on the 'triumphal result' of their 1840 decision to abandon paddle wheels in favour of the largely untried screw propulsion. Writing on 17 December 1844, he said the ship had been completely under the control of her helm and that much more steam could have been generated if required.

The official trials began in January and were remarkably successful for a totally new concept in marine machinery. During a 95-mile run in the Bristol Channel, the ship averaged more than 11 knots, with a top speed of 12½ knots in short bursts. The vessel performed precisely to specification and no need was seen for any alterations, despite the fact that she was as different from all other vessels afloat as the first jet aircraft had been from the piston-engined machines of the day.

On 23 January 1845 the *Great Britain* left Bristol for Blackwall on the Thames for final furbishment of the interior. On this trip she was tested to the utmost in heavy seas; at one stage the ship was brought to a standstill by the impact of the waves and minor damage was caused. But she kept on course throughout the following day until the storm abated. The heaviest weather was experienced off Lundy Island and J. Walter, a celebrated marine artist of the day, preserved the dramatic scene (see page 24).

In the mid-afternoon of 26 January the *Great Britain* moored in the Thames, creating a huge sensation. Her extraordinary length and bizarre appearance attracted attention the entire length of London's river. For Brunel and his colleagues, however, the pleasure was in the performance of the engines which had averaged 10 knots overall, with a peak performance in excess of 13. The first full voyage of a modern steamship had been a total success; iron was now king, or soon would be.

The country's scribes and poets took the new ship to their hearts. As one anonymous poetaster put it in that year:

Six masts—like princely sons to bear!
'Great Britain' for my name
My smoke trail black on the sun bright air
My screw as swift and my sails as fair
As the trumpet voice of Fame!

The passengers' quarters in the *Great Britain* naturally attracted considerable public attention as the time approached for her maiden voyage to New York. The rear area, behind the machinery amidships, was reserved for first-class passengers who could theoretically number 120. The lower of two decks was the dining saloon, with cabins outboard on both sides. Above this was the promenade deck, again with cabins to both port and starboard. Second-class accommodation, forward of the engine room, was arranged in a similar fashion with the promenade deck and cabins above the dining area and further passenger accommodation. The ship in her original guise could carry 132 second-class passengers, bringing the total in both classes to a possible 252.

These contemporary drawings in the *Illustrated London News* are invaluable records of the vessel as she must have appeared to visitors in London during the early weeks of 1845. Some artistic licence must be admitted, however, as both the dining and promenade areas were less spacious than the small human figures would suggest. Headroom was only 6ft 6in on the promenade deck and 7ft 6in in the dining saloons. Cargo and coal was stored forward and accommodation for both officers and crew was arranged in the forward part of the ship.

The early months of 1845 were a time of public adulation for the directors of the Great Western Steamship Company whose creation was attracting a succession of VIP visitors to the Thames. But the more astute minds on the board were grappling with the commercial realities that lay ahead. Would the new liner be as lucrative a proposition as they had dreamed five years earlier?

The ship had cost almost £120,000 and the accounting practices of the day suggested that almost a quarter of this sum—£30,000—should be written off each year for depreciation, insurance, interest charges and so on. Wages for the 130 officers and men would claim about £9,000, coal perhaps £12,000 and management charges a further £10,000. Thus there would be perhaps £61,000 on the debit side of the ledger.

Assuming seven round trips to New York each year, the income could be a theoretical £100,000 from passengers and a further £35,000 from cargo (assuming full bookings in each case). Although no one could have expected to run at full capacity, there was still sufficient potential in the ship to make her a very profitable venture. But fate was to intervene and the company was not to reap the benefits of its great enterprise.

The modern reconstruction at the top of the page shows how the *Great Britain* looked (starboard elevation) on her 1845 maiden voyage to New York. The square sails could not normally be turned to the extent shown and are depicted in a convention to demonstrate their shape and comparative size. Current restoration work on the ship in Bristol is aimed at restoring her to this appearance. The artist's view (*below*) is of the vessel as she was after her first refit in 1846, again from the starboard elevation. Note the disappearance of the mast behind the funnel and the greater sail area.

These modern illustrations give a realistic impression of life aboard the ship in 1845. (*Below*) The weather deck looking forward, showing clearly the functional simplicity of the original design. (*Upper right*) The first-class promenade deck looking aft of the midship line along to the sloping square windows of the transom. Along each side are cabins and state-rooms. Between the doors are light boxes which pass light from the weather deck skylights through to the dining saloon deck below.

(*Bottom right*) The view on the first-class dining saloon deck, looking aft of the midship line. Again, cabins and state-rooms are positioned down each side, the area between being taken up with three long tables with fixed benches. The colours used in the *Great Britain* were subtle shades—pale lemons, blues, white and gold—and the artists have followed careful contemporary descriptions.

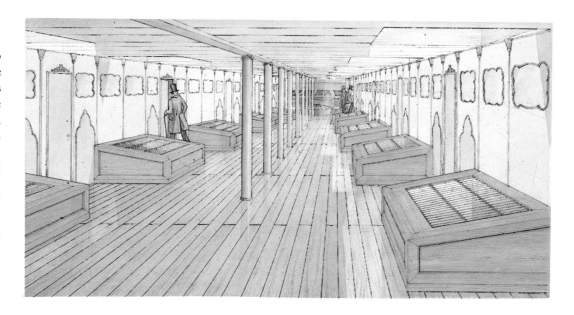

The high spot of the vessel's five-month stay in the Thames was a visit by Queen Victoria and Prince Albert on 23 April 1845. The royal party travelled up river from Greenwich Palace, preceded by a state barge bearing London's Lord Mayor and followed by an armada of river steamers. According to contemporary accounts, the Queen was astonished by the length of the vessel and, in particular, by the size of the immense chain which turned the screw shaft. On leaving she told Captain James Hosken: 'I am very much gratified with the sight of your magnificent ship and I wish you every possible success on your voyages across the Atlantic.' The vessel was then moved to the East India Dock where she was thrown open to the people of London throughout the whole of May. Then, on 12 June, she left for Liverpool to begin her working life.

THE "GREAT BRITAIN" STEAM-SHIP.

Our illustration shows this leviathan steam-ship leaving Blackwall, on the afternoon of Thursday, the 12th inst. The hour named for her starting was three o'clock, but she did not cast off her moorings until full half-past four o'clock, when, a strong hawser from her starboard bow having been attached to the *Ariel*, Woolwich steam-boat, which had a large party on board, to accompany her as far as Sea Reach, she was towed clear of the huge mooring buoy, and then proceeded at a very steady pace in the middle of the stream down the river. On her several masts were hoisted the English white ensign, and the American, French, Belgian, and Russian colours; and as she slowly passed the Brunswick-pier, she was loudly cheered by the assembled multitude. On passing Woolwich, it seemed as if the whole population had turned out to behold her. The Dockyard was lined with the naval and military officers connected with that depôt, whose cheers were loud, long, and continued, and which were as heartily returned by the passengers and crew. Near Erith the tide turned, and the expanse of water being larger, her rate was increased considerably, and she passed Gravesend shortly after seven o'clock, with a strong tide that would carry her well out to sea. Throughout her whole progress down the river she was hailed in the most gratifying manner; and the rapid speed of her screw propeller, unaccompanied by any apparent agitation of the water, notwithstanding her huge dimensions, rendered her progress peculiarly interesting. She had on board about eighty passengers for a trip round the coast. She will start from Liverpool, on the 26th of July, on her first trip across the Atlantic. She reached Cowes on Friday, left at nine next morning, and entered Plymouth Sound at eight p.m. In the passage, her average speed was about 11 miles an hour. From London to Plymouth she was 33 hours under steam. During the whole of her voyage the weather was more or less hazy. From Blackwall, she conveyed about 75 passengers to Cowes. where 40 landed. At that port she took on board 20, and took in all about 60 to Plymouth. Her expected arrival here had long been an object of great interest to the inhabitants of Devon and Cornwall, and early in the forenoon the hills by the sea-side were studded with anxious spectators. Owing to the thickness of the weather, when first descried she was within the Mew-stone. The preconcerted signal of rigning St. Andrew's Church bells induced the inhabitants of this great naval port to rush in crowds towards the shores of the Sound. The Hoe was densely covered, and the western Hoe, veen to the edges of its precipitous limestone quarries, was deeply fringed with persons of both sexes and all ages, who heartily cheered the iron wonder.

Outside the Breakwater she was boarded by Mr. W. Walker, the Queen's Harbour-master, who skilfully piloted her by the eastern channel into the Sound, through which she threaded her way among the numerous yachts, steam and sailing vessels, gigs, shore-boats, &c., attracted there by her arrival. Passing to the northward of Drake's Island, she entered Firestone Bay, and in about six minutes turned completely round, through Barnpool, and afterwards majestically entered Millbay.

The expectations of nautical men at Plymouth have been fully realised on seeing this extraordinary ship. When first observed, stem on, she did not appear so formidable, but, when presenting her broadside to view, all expressed their surprise at the symmetrical appearance of the great reality. The manner in which she answered her helm was a peculiar cause for admiration.

THE GREAT BRITAIN STEAM-SHIP, LEAVING BLACKWALL.

This report in the *Illustrated London News* chronicled the *Great Britain*'s passage from London to Liverpool in June 1845. As the reporter observed in the careful language of the day: 'The rapid speed of her screw propeller, unaccompanied by any apparent agitation of the water, notwithstanding her huge dimensions, rendered her progress peculiarly interesting.' At Plymouth the expectations of nautical men had been fully realised: 'When first observed, stem on, she did not appear so formidable but, when presenting her broadside to view, all expressed their surprise at the symmetrical appearance of the great reality.'

From Plymouth she went to Dublin and then to Liverpool where some 2,500 people a day poured over the ship, delaying preparations for her maiden voyage across the Atlantic. It was not until the afternoon of 26 July 1845 that she was able to leave the Mersey for New York—and even then there were trippers aboard for the first few miles.

23

The illustrations on this and the facing page, though similar, are separated by more than a year. J. Walter's famous painting of the *Great Britain* in heavy seas at 3.00pm on 23 January 1845 was published as a print by Messrs Ackermann & Company of London and it sold well. The next year the ship underwent her first refit, which included the scrapping of the mast behind the funnel, and Ackermann obliged by re-issuing the heavy seas painting (*below*) with only five masts! Whether Mr Walter did the retouching job and was paid for it we do not know.

The other features of the 1846 refit were the installation of a four-bladed propeller instead of the original six-bladed affair, improvements in the boilers, the replacement of the original wire rigging by hemp, largely to please the traditionalists, and an increase in the size of the fourth mast (now the third) with additional sail area.

The ship left for New York on 26 July 1845 on the first Atlantic crossing by a screw steamship. Thousands of spectators lined the banks of the Mersey to see her off. Only 45 people had been brave enough to book berths, although there was a good cargo of 360 tons.

The voyage, in bad weather, took 14½ days, an extremely good time. In New York the *Great Britain* attracted the same attention and admiration as British cities had given her. 'Grand and beautiful', was the verdict of the

New York Herald. So great was the public interest that the Great Western Steamship Company charged 25 cents to tour the vessel and turned the proceeds from 21,000 visitors over to charity.

The *Great Britain* made only four round voyages to New York in 1845 and 1846. During the winter of 1846 she was refitted in a more efficient guise and looked set for a long and lucrative career on the Atlantic route.

The British in Victorian times had an almost religious feeling for steam, and Isambard Kingdom Brunel (*far right*) was the high priest of the cult which was to restore the country's dominance of the world's merchant fleets after the early nineteenth-century supremacy of the Americans. He was born in 1806, the son of Sir Marc Brunel, a royalist Frenchman who left his country after the revolution and came to Britain via the United States.

During his 53 years Brunel built 25 railways in Britain, Ireland, Italy and India; 130 bridges (five of them suspension), eight piers and harbour systems and three ocean-going steamships. He died in 1859 worn out by his exertions in building his most awesome creation, the *Great Eastern*. This mammoth iron ship was 692ft long against the 322ft of the *Great Britain*, contained more than seven times as much iron, and had a maximum displacement of 25,000 tons. She had a chequered career spread over 30 years, was a failure as a passenger liner, but performed yeoman service all over the world as a cable-layer.

Second only to Brunel, the *Great Britain* meant one man to tens of thousands of passengers on the Australian run: John Gray (*above right*), captain of the ship from 1854 to 1872. A Shetlander by birth he was immensely popular: as was once remarked, 'the beau ideal of a merchant captain—brave, skilful, manly and resourceful'.

Francis Pettit Smith, then farming at Hendon, north of London, took out a patent for the screw propeller in May 1836 and is thus another key figure in our story. He hit upon the idea after trials with a model boat on his farm pond. Pettit Smith is pictured (*below right*) in the centre of a group of the *Great Britain*'s officers in 1852.

When Brunel and his colleagues were building the *Great Western* and then her iron successor, the Americans were dominant in the Atlantic. Their fine sailing clippers were economical and ran to tight and reliable schedules. From the 1840s onwards, the scene was transformed with Britain fighting the once dominant yankees, not with wood and canvas but with new ideas and materials. The scene above captures this challenge: the *Great Britain* is returning to Liverpool from her first voyage to New York. On the right is the *Victoria*, launched in 1844 and perhaps the most famous US clipper of her day. It is tradition versus modernity, with the old and new world roles curiously reversed.

The Evening Mirror.

VOLUME II.—NUMBER 252.   NEW-YORK, MONDAY EVENING, AUGUST 11, 1845.   SINGLE COPIES TWO CENTS.

THE "GREAT BRITAIN" STEAM-SHIP, NEWLY RIGGED.

"THE GREAT BRITAIN" STEAM-SHIP.

This magnificent steam-ship sailed from Liverpool on Monday morning, for New York, carrying out 28 passengers and a large cargo. She passed down the Mersey in splendid style, and at a speed not surpassed by the finest sea-going steamers; thus proving the whole of the alterations made in her since her last voyage, to be decidedly beneficial.

These new fittings are thus described in the *Manchester Guardian*. They include another screw, and masts and spars of a somewhat different character from those under which the *Great Britain* has four times crossed the Atlantic, and which are decidedly more in accordance with nautical notions. Her propeller, which is of immense strength, and weighs seven tons, has four vanes, each of great width; her former one had six, but of less width. The diameter of the propeller, from tip to tip of the opposite vanes, is the same as before —15 feet 6 inches. Her masts are now five in number, the whole of which are stepped upon the kelson, and fitted with rope rigging. In her previous voyages, the *Great Britain* had six masts, fitted with wire rigging; and all, with the exception of the mainmast, were stepped upon deck; and, therefore, admitted of her being lowered at the pleasure of her commander. This it was thought might have proved an advantage when steaming a succession of contrary gales; but, experience soon proved that such an advantage was more than counterbalanced by attendant evils, which it is not necessary now to enlarge upon. Having five masts, her style of rig does not admit a nautical cognomen; but we will attempt a description of it by comparison:—15 yards, or thereabouts, forward of the unnel (which is itself 20 feet forward of the centre of the vessel) stands the mainmast; which, instead of bearing aloft a single topmast, as formerly, carries a maintopmast and topgallant mast, with their respective spars—similar in every respect, only of greater bulk, to those of the mainmast of one of the largest Atlantic liners. Abaft the funnel, about 20 yards, stands a similar mast, less bulky, perhaps, but of the same height, and fitted just as the one previously described. Her foremast and fourth and fifth masts, with the exception of being stepped upon the kelson, present the same outward characteristics as the old ones, and carry the same description of sails—spencers. With her old style of rig, the *Great Britain* behaved well under the canvass; she made part of her last homeward passage entirely without the aid of steam, in consequence of her propeller having been shattered so as to be rendered useless She even then, under great disadvantages, outsailed two or three liners she fell in with, and frequently accomplished 10 and 11 knots per hour.

In an experimental trip, made on the 30th ult., the *Great Britain* beat the Cork steamer *Nimrod*, and the mail steamer *Prince*, about an hour; and she held way for about half an hour with the fast new ron steamer *Sea-King*.

There are other improved points in the *Great Britain's* new fittings; her boilers give ample steam without any difficulty, with easy firing, and the consumption of coals is much lessened. The alterations in the pumps, valves, &c., have answered every expectation, and the screw is beyond doubt better than the old one. The highest speed in the above trip (steam alone) was 11½ nautical, or about 13½ statute miles per hour, the engines at the time making 16½ revolutions.

Our Engraving of the newly-rigged vessel is from a clever sketch by Mr. J. Walter, the marine artist, of Bristol.

THE STEAM SHIP GREAT BRITAIN.

This mammoth of the ocean, which sailed from Liverpool on her first trip to this country on Saturday, the twenty-sixth of July, is destined to create as much excitement here, as she has done in England and Ireland, where a premium was offered to the proprietors, for the purpose of inducing them to cross the Irish channel. In Liverpool, upwards of 33000 persons visited her, during her nine days in the dock, and in London, we should suppose, it almost impossible to calculate the number. Doubtless, there will be a rush here, and we hope the agents will make such arrangements, as will enable our citizens to gratify themselves with a view of this long expected curiosity.

The launching of this magnificent vessel was an era in naval architecture, and her first voyage across the Atlantic will form another of little less importance—her several experimental trips were highly successful, and the report of her worthy and experienced Captain Hosken will be looked with deep interest. We find the following description of her in an old English paper.

THE STEAMSHIP GREAT BRITAIN.—This magnificent vessel, which was launched last week, at Bristol, is composed entirely of iron, and is the largest ever built since the days of Noah. There are no paddle wheels or boxes, the Archimedian screw being used. Her burthen is 3,600 tons, being 2,000 tons more than that of the Great Western. She will be propelled by engines of 1000-horse power combined.

The following are her dimensions:—Length from figure head to taffrail, 322 feet; length of keel, 289 feet, extreme width, 50 feet 6 inches; she has four decks, the upper deck is flush, and is 308 feet long; the second deck consists of two promenade saloons, the aft or first 110 feet six inches by 22 feet, and the forward, or second class, 67 feet by 21 feet 9 inches. The third deck consists of the dining saloons, the grand saloon measuring 96 feet 6 inches, by 30 feet, and the second class 61 feet by 21 feet 9 inches. The whole of the saloons are 8 feet 3 inches high, and surrounded by sleeping berths, of which there are 26, with single beds, and 113 containing two, giving 252 berths. This large number is exclusive of the accommodation which could be prepared on the numerous sofas. The fourth deck is appropriated for the reception of cargo, of which 1,200 will be carried in addition to 1,000 tons of coal. The forecastle is intended for the officers' and sailors' mess rooms and sleeping berths, with the sail-rooms underneath. The engines and boilers occupy a space of 80 feet in the middle portion of the vessel. The engine-room and the cooking establishment are situate in this part of the ship.— There are three boilers; these are heated by twenty-four fires, and will contain 200 tons of water.

There are four engines of 250 horse power each, the cylinders of which are 7 feet 4 inches in diameter. The chimney is 30 feet high, and 8 feet diameter. She is fitted with six masts, the highest of which is 74 feet above deck.

The quantity of canvass carried will be about 1700 square yards; she will be fitted with the patent wire rigging; the hull is divided into four water-tight compartments, and the quantity of coal consumed will be about 60 tons per day; upwards of 1500 tons of iron have been used in her construction and that of the engines and boilers; the draught of water when laden will be 16 feet, and the displacement about 3,200 tons; the plates of the keel are from one inch to three quarters of an inch thick, and the other plates are about half an inch thick; she is double riveted throughout; the ribs are formed of angel iron 6 in. by 3 1-2 in. by 1-2 an in. at the bottom of the vessel, and 7-16ths thicks at the top; the mean distance of the ribs are 14 in. from centre to centre. The ship will be fitted with very powerful pumps, which can throw off 7,000 gallons of water per minute.

Stranded in Dundrum Bay: the ship survived but the Great Western Steamship Company died as a result of the disaster.

The fifth voyage of the *Great Britain* started well. She left Liverpool at 11.00am on 22 September 1846, carrying 180 passengers and her normal complement of 130 crew under Captain Hosken, a former Royal Navy officer. But that evening she was aground, stranded in Dundrum Bay on the Northern Ireland coast. Her captain had apparently missed the vital lighthouse on the Isle of Man, and had carried on course until the Dundrum Bay light, by which time it was too late to avoid the coast. Her passengers were rescued the next morning, carried off in carts normally used for seaweed manure, and the ship was driven further up the shore to protect her from the winter gales.

The directors of the Great Western Steamship Company accepted Captain Hosken's statement that admiralty sea charts were to blame for being inaccurate; others, however, were of a different opinion. The stranding was 'beyond all possibility of doubt the most egregious blundering' thundered the *Mechanics Magazine* in December 1846. Whoever was to blame, the stranding was to mark the end of the company and the start of a very different life for the *Great Britain*. For nearly a year, the great iron ship lay stranded at Dundrum Bay.

Breakwaters were constructed around the vessel to try to protect her from the storms. Twice, the breakwaters were smashed to pieces. Brunel managed to visit the ship in December, and was appalled by what he saw—the ship 'lying like a useless saucepan kicking about on the most exposed shore you can imagine'.

Under instructions from Brunel, an effective breakwater was constructed by Alexander Bremner, a Scottish salvage expert. It was built of beech saplings, which bent with the force of the waves 'like the trees of the forest in a gale of wind . . . Not only a handsome object but an exceedingly efficient one', an admiring journalist reported.

It protected her all winter, and in the spring of 1847 serious attempts to rescue her began. All the stores, furniture and fittings were removed, so that she was half her weight when she had gone aground. Under Bremner's directions, teams of Irish navvies built trenches beneath her. The bottom of the ship was repaired where it had been holed in two places.

The actual raising of the vessel was achieved by attaching great boxes of sand, each weighing 30 tons, to the forward end of the ship, working on pulleys. When full, the boxes tended to lift the ship. It was an immensely improbable plan, which worked. On 27 August 1847, the *Great Britain* moved. 'Huzza! Huzza! You know what that means . . .', Captain Claxton wrote to Brunel that day, 'I have no doubt that tomorrow we shall see her free.' He was right; on the 28th the ship limped back to Liverpool.

The Great Western Steamship Company put her up for auction in September 1847; they had no alternative. The ship had been insured for only £17,000, one-seventh of her cost; the directors had been forced to sell the *Great Western* in April of that year and they had no other source of revenue. The ship had a reserve price of just £40,000, but bidding reached only half that figure. So she lay as she was, unused, in Liverpool for more than three years.

The ship was sold finally in December 1850 to Gibbs, Bright & Co for just £18,000. Extensive alterations were made; new engines (*right*) installed, made by John Penn & Co and described by the *Illustrated London News* as 'of the most beautiful workmanship, and a credit to their constructors'. One more mast was removed and new twin funnels were fitted.

A long deck house was built above the top deck, 300ft long and 7ft 6in high, increasing passenger capacity to 50 first class and 680 others. The first-class dining saloon is pictured above. By April 1852 the ship was ready to sail, and left for New York on a successful shakedown cruise on 1 May.

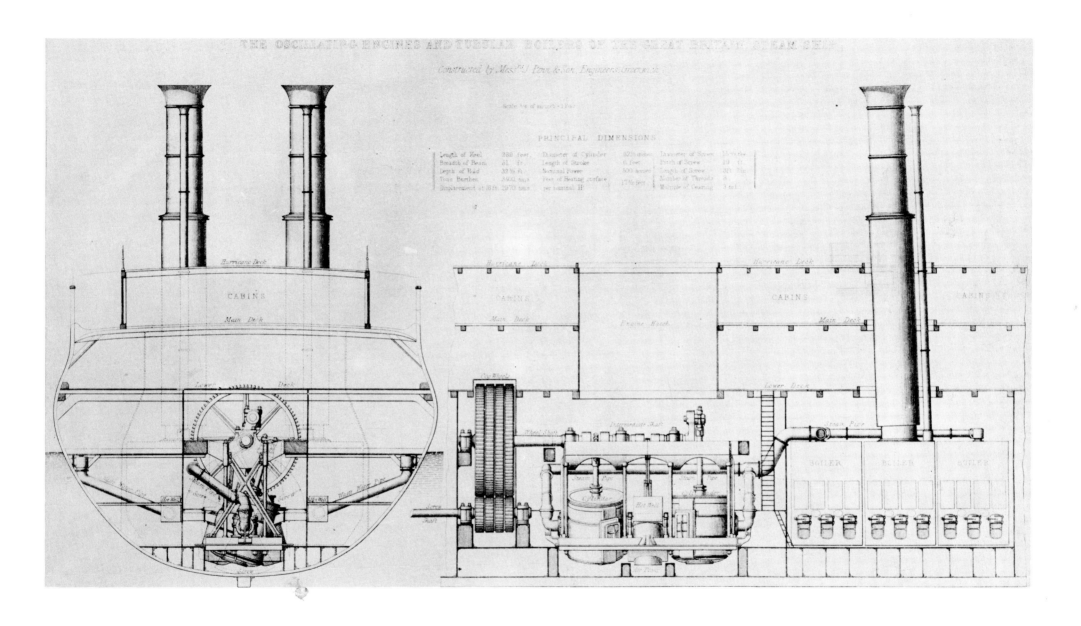

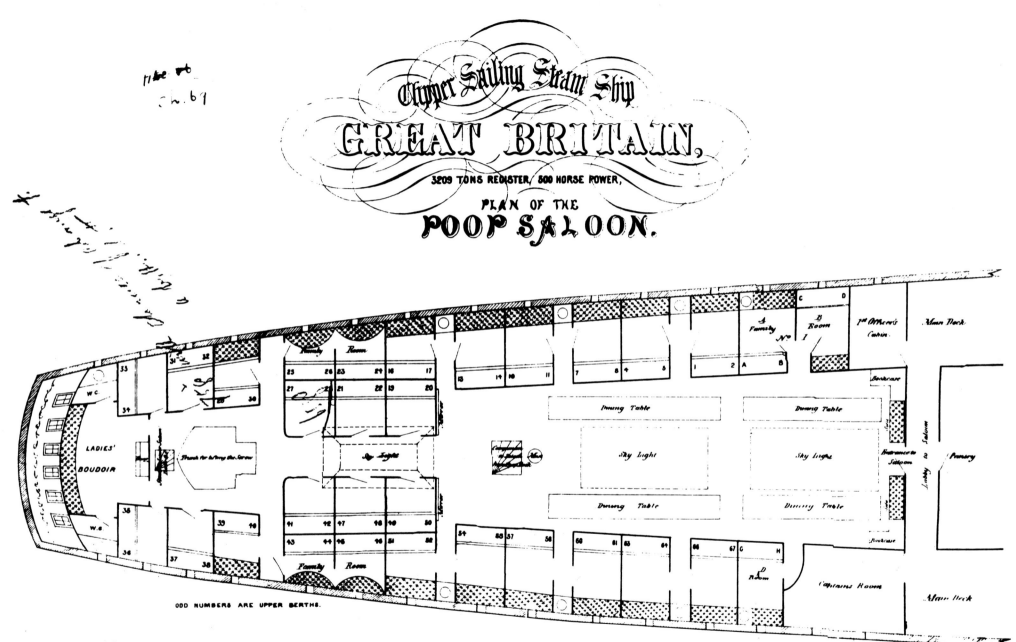

Clipper Sailing Steam Ship
GREAT BRITAIN,
3209 TONS REGISTER, 500 HORSE POWER,
PLAN OF THE
POOP SALOON.

ODD NUMBERS ARE UPPER BERTHS.

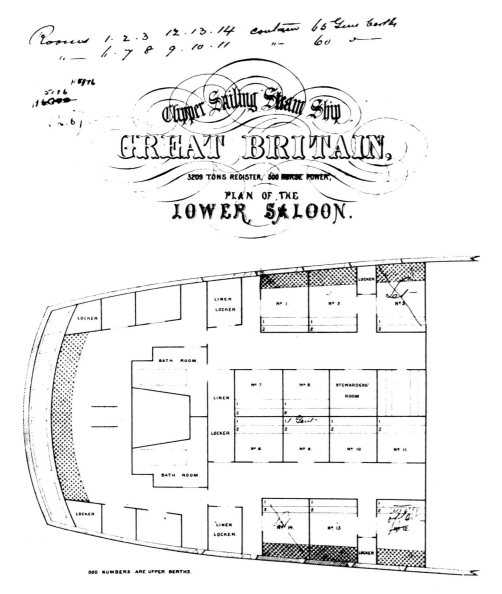

Rooms 1. 2. 3 12. 13. 14 contain 65 First berths
" — 1. 7. 8. 9. 10. 11 " — 60 "

Clipper Sailing Steam Ship
GREAT BRITAIN,
3209 TONS REGISTER, 500 HORSE POWER,
PLAN OF THE
LOWER SALOON.

ODD NUMBERS ARE UPPER BERTHS.

The deckhouse introduced in 1852 and referred to on page 34 provided more comfortable accommodation in a vessel about to begin a series of long voyages in hot climates. On this page and at left are booking plans showing the location of the new berths for first-class passengers on the poop deck and the lower saloon beneath.

A VISIT TO THE ENGINE ROOM.

A SHORT account of what we saw and learnt the other day down in the engine-room, may be a source of information to those of your readers who have not had an opportunity of "doing the lions" in these lower regions of our little world, a department occupying the whole depth of the vessel amidships, and measuring alone more than one-third of her tonnage.

Entering at the door on the main deck, we descend by an iron ladder to the first flat, a gallery around which are situated the engineers' rooms. Descending another flight of iron steps, we find ourselves in the immediate presence of the engines, to which our attention is now directed, the eye being attracted by the two powerful pistons as they rise and fall in their mysterious sockets. There are two complete engines (both of the same dimensions, and alike in every respect) employed in driving the screw. These two engines, which are considered two of the finest afloat, are on the oscillating principle, which is now being adopted on nearly all first-class steamships; the cylinders are 82½ inches diameter, and the length of stroke 6 feet. To work the engines there are six boilers, each boiler having three furnaces—eighteen furnaces in all. At present, however, only four of the boilers are used; the engines not being wrought up to full speed. The boilers occupy the *stoke-hole*, or fore part of the engine-room; they are all separate from each other, and are on the tubular principle, each containing, we understand, 280 brass tubes. They are each 11 feet long by 13 feet deep.

Adjoining the boiler room is the coal depot and store room, which contains, in addition to the necessary stores of grease, &c., nearly all the parts of another engine in case of any break-down happening to those in use. In a little workshop over one of the boilers we observe the blacksmith hard at work (as blacksmiths always are) repairing some implements of firemen's craft. Retracing our steps we come to the screw shaft, which is connected to the engine by means of cogwheels. The wheel on the screw shaft is one third the diameter of that on the engine shaft, consequently the screw makes three revolutions for one stroke of the piston. We can form, then, an idea of the rate at which the screw revolves, when we know that the piston—when at full speed—makes about 20 strokes per minute.

The shaft, which is 105 feet in length and weighs 24 tons, runs along a narrow passage in the bottom of the ship, right aft to the screw. Down this dark alley we are guided by the light of an oil lamp into the small chamber at the farther end, where the shaft fits into a square hole in the screw. When the screw is to be taken up, the shaft is withdrawn, telescope fashion; an engineer, with five men, being in attendance for this purpose. Communication is here held with the deck by a speaking tube and bell. The propeller is hung in a frame outside, which is fitted on to the stern post like a window-frame, and it is this frame, with the screw attached, which we see drawn up or lowered by the chain from the capstan. But we have been long enough in this dismal submarine passage, which, with the shaft whirling alongside of us, is rather too much for our nerves. Before leaving the shaft, however, we must notice the pump, which, by being joined to it, can at any time be set to work to pump the ship; a great saving of labour this must prove to the crew, were such a duty to become necessary. There are numerous other items which ought to be noticed in the course of our short sketch did space permit, such as the condenser, a distillery in connection with this department, for the manufacture of the best of all liquors, fresh water, which it is capable of supplying to the extent of 1,500 gallons per diem; the telegraph, which is used by the commander on deck when giving orders to the engineers below; the register, an ingenious apparatus for indicating the number of revolutions of the screw during the voyage, &c., &c.; but we have already occupied too much of your valuable space.

THE "GREAT BRITAIN" STEAM-SHIP LEAVING PRINCE'S PIER, LIVERPOOL, FOR AUSTRALIA.

DEPARTURE OF THE "GREAT BRITAIN" FOR AUSTRALIA.

ABOUT three o'clock on Saturday afternoon, this splendid screw steam-ship, Captain Mathews, weighed her anchor in the Sloyne, and steamed gently down towards the mouth of the Mersey; her passage being watched with intense interest by crowds of enthusiastic spectators, who had stationed themselves on the Liverpool side. Steam-boats and other craft, gaily dressed with flags and streamers, and filled with people, were moving about in all directions, while the ferry-boats were crammed with passengers, who preferred the Cheshire side of the river as a point of view. The deck of the *Great Britain* was crowded with passengers, to take farewell of old England. Several tug-boats hovered round the leviathan; at intervals guns were fired from the *Great Britain* herself; from the *Arctic*, which lay in the Sloyne; and from Mr. Parry's pleasure gardens at Seacombe, while an almost uninterrupted series of hearty cheers resounded from the steamer, the neighbouring boats, and the piers. At length the fort was breasted, and after firing a salute the smaller vessels fell back, and the *Great Britain* sped on her way with upwards of 630 passengers and a very heavy mail.

The *Great Britain*, at the time she left the river, was drawing 22 feet of water. The quantity of coal taken on board is about 1400 tons, chiefly Welsh, with a small quantity of anthracite and patent fuel, as an experiment. There is enough to steam the whole distance without stopping; but, lest anything should occur, she will call at the Cape of Good Hope to replenish her supply, and take in live stock. It is expected that she will reach the Cape in about twenty-five days, whither ships have been dispatched with coals to wait her arrival. After staying there two or three days, she will proceed to Melbourne and Sydney, and it is confidently expected that she will reach the former place in fifty-six days from England; whereas double that length of time is considered an average voyage for a sailing vessel. The *Great Britain* is fully equipped to resist any attempt to attack the vessel that might be made, for she is mounted with six heavy deck guns, and arms and ammunition for 100 men. The crew of the *Great Britain* consists of about 130 persons in all.

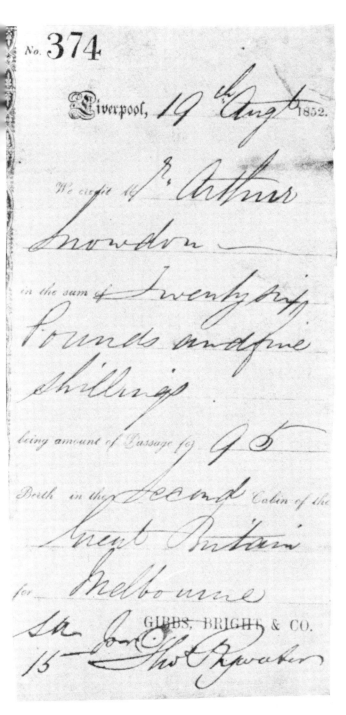

This receipt was issued for a ticket to Arthur Snowdon on the ship's first voyage to Australia. He was a successful migrant, became Mayor of Melbourne and was knighted in 1895. His grandson presented this receipt to the ship's museum in Bristol.

The *Great Britain* then embarked upon the most successful period in her history. For a quarter of a century she sailed to and from Australia, carrying emigrants from all Europe to a new life in the colonies and more particularly to the mines that had sprung up after the first discovery of gold in the state of Victoria in 1850.

In all, the ship made 32 round trips to Australia. Her routes took her around the world: out by the west coast of Africa, around the Cape of Good Hope and thence to Melbourne; sometimes back by Cape Horn and home along the eastern seaboard of the Americas.

Voyages on average took 65 days. The *Dublin Telegraph* in 1854, at the end of her second voyage to Australia, declared: 'Her late performances prove her to be by far the fleetest ship in the world.' After a further refit in 1853 which converted her to a sailing ship with auxiliary steam rather than the other way round, and with a commander who understood her capabilities, she proved remarkably consistent in the length of her voyages: nearly 70 per cent were completed in 65 days or less.

The ship first sailed for Australia from Liverpool on 21 August 1852 at 3.00pm. Crowds of enthusiastic spectators watched her leave, and the decks of the ship were thronged with 630 passengers for their last view of England. The first voyage was not an unqualified success. It turned out to be a long one: 81 days. The Captain, Robert Matthews, was not a popular man, and within a fortnight of sailing passengers had got together to complain about the bad food and the irregularity of meals.

The route that Matthews decided to take on this voyage would have been sensible for a full-powered steam ship. As it was, the *Great Britain* ran out of coal after days spent steaming against the trade winds, and had to put back to St Helena, involving a diversion of 2,000 miles, to take on more coal which had to be bought at an exorbitant price.

Finally the ship arrived in Melbourne on 12 November. For all the troubles on the voyage she had a wonderful welcome, and this was repeated when the ship sailed around the coast to Sydney. Returning to Melbourne to begin the journey home, the *Great Britain* staged a memorable grand ball for 400 local citizens on her decks.

The return voyage to Liverpool was faster and less eventful, and in April 1853 she was laid up for a thorough refit.

Australia bound: the *Great Britain* drops her pilot at Liverpool Bar in August 1852.

The first voyage to Australia had shown that the ship (as pictured here) did not have sufficiently powerful engines to operate solely, or even mainly, as a steam ship. The sailing arrangements had to be improved. The last of Brunel's 'fore and aft' masts were removed and the total number of masts reduced to three—all conventional ones which were more efficient and gave a better balanced rig than previously. One of the main influences on the choice of new rigging was the ship's second officer, who had joined just before the start of the first Australian voyage—John Gray.

The *Great Britain* sailed again in August 1853 with 319 passengers on board and 600 tons of cargo. Her 34 first-class passengers had paid up to 70 guineas for the trip; second-class tickets were '42 guineas and a few at 25 guineas'. A later sailing bill dating from 1861 shows the fares for third-class passengers to be between 18 and 20 guineas with steerage at 14 and 16 guineas.

The ship arrived in Melbourne on 15 October 1853, a voyage of 65 days. This must have been a relief to the owners, as they had contracted to carry the 600 tons of freight in a time of 65 days or less—with a penalty of £2 a ton for every day's delay. Considering the price for carrying the freight had been just £8 a ton, their entire income from this source could have been wiped out by four days' delay.

On Christmas Eve the ship left again for Liverpool where she arrived after a voyage of only 62 days. The cargo on this voyage had included seven tons of gold and 23 bales of cotton, the first of the latter ever to be imported from Australia. One of the passengers also brought back an unusual item: the body of his wife, who had died on board, preserved in a cask of vinegar. At the

bound together with iron bands. These masts were to survive to the end of her working life; indeed, they were only taken down for the ship's final return to England in 1970.

The ship now had a quarter more sail than previously—33,000sq ft in all—double the original 1845 sail area. The scale of this can be judged from the fact that more than 50 miles of rigging were now required. The passenger quarters were improved and increased by extending the long deckhouse right to the stern; 84 first-class passengers could now be carried. Evidently, little expense, particularly in the first-class quarters, had been spared. In February 1857, *The Engineer* stated that 'nothing can be conceived more perfect than the fittings of the ship. Her saloon is not excelled for the simplicity and elegance of its colouring and its adornments are extremely handsome.'

Improvements in the engines were also made, and a single oval funnel replaced the twin funnels fitted in 1851. A special lifting screw, which could be used effectively without interfering with the ship's sailing capabilities, was fitted. The success of these arrangements can be judged by the fact that the *Great Britain* continued in this form without a major refit for a further 18 years.

The ship sailed again for Melbourne in February 1857 and arrived home again in August. Once again war service intervened; in October of that year she sailed to Bombay carrying troops to deal with the Indian Mutiny. A trip to New York followed, and then the ship settled down in earnest on the Australian route from November 1858.

end of this voyage, Captain Matthews retired. On 20 April 1854 John Gray became her captain, the start of a long and satisfactory association for both the ship and the man.

The Australian run was interrupted on two occasions when the ship was chartered by the Government for war service. In the early 1850s, she had the distinction of causing two invasion scares, once in Liverpool and once in Melbourne. Firing off rockets or guns in celebration of her arrival home, rumour spread that 'the Russians were sure to be coming up the river, and hundreds ran down . . . to get a glimpse of the grisly "Bear of the North" ', the *Dublin Weekly Telegraph* reported. A few months later in Melbourne, the

Great Britain's celebration gun salutes brought out a rapidly formed cavalry who galloped towards the bay, backed up by infantry armed with sticks and pick handles.

In 1855, however, the ship entered the Crimean War in earnest. At the end of her third voyage to Australia she was fitted out to carry 1,650 troops and 30 horses. For 15 months she sailed to and from the Crimea, calling at the ports of Gibraltar, Marseilles, Malta and Balaclava. In all, she transported about 45,000 troops.

In the summer of 1856 the ship was once again put in for a complete refit. Her sailing rig was changed completely; three new massive masts were fitted, each made from four tree trunks

The weather through which the *Great Britain* sailed ranged from tropical heat to snowstorms. One of the hazards she regularly encountered was icebergs. In 1854 she passed a vast iceberg island, 50 miles in breadth and 15ft high, which was to prove fatal to another British ship, the sailing vessel *Guiding Star*, a few weeks later. She was

THE GREAT BRITAIN AMONG THE ICEBERGS NEAR
CAPE HORN.

THE screw-steamer Great Britain, which arrived at Liverpool on the 26th ult., having made the passage from Melbourne in the short period of sixty-one days, passed through an extraordinary drift of icebergs on the 12th of September and two or three following days, in the neighbourhood of Cape Horn. We have been favoured by Mr. G. T. Horne, one of the passengers, with a sketch of one of the groups of icebergs and with a set of drawings which represent the fantastic shapes of each iceberg separately ; but while the latter may be worthy of inspection for the sake of their scientific interest, we have preferred the general view shown in our Engraving. Ninety-five icebergs were seen on the first day, but the total number counted was 212. Sometimes the vessel passed a group of ten or twelve thickly crowded together. A very heavy sea was running, and the wind blew almost a gale, with snow-squalls every few minutes, and clouds as black as night. A small printed paper, entitled "The Great Britain Chronicle," which was edited by Mr. Hatton, another passenger, during the voyage, reports the occurrence of this phenomenon a fortnight after sailing from Hobson's Bay. "It is a wonderful sight," observes the journalist, "just like Dover cliffs floating along. We are surrounded by a complete sea of ice. Passed eighty-three icebergs altogether to-day. Captain Gray is very anxious ; he and three mates and four men on the look-out ; I think him a first-rate seaman." We may here remark that, towards the end of the voyage, Captain Gray, Lieutenant of the Royal Naval Reserve, who has been commander of the Great Britain for ten years past, received from the passengers a gratifying testimonial of their esteem. Mr. Petersen and the other officers of the ship, including Dr. Alexander, the surgeon, were likewise thanked by those who had been under their care.

wrecked on the ice cliffs with 180 emigrants on board. The *Great Britain* could, of course, steam out of any difficulties, and the ice became just another sight for passengers: 'About half past four on Saturday last', reported the *Great Britain Times* in 1865, 'those who had never seen an iceberg before, had this pleasure gratified'.

In 1861 the *Great Britain* made her contribution to sport history by carrying the first All England XI to Australia to challenge the colonials on the cricket field. It was also a unique event in that the tour was sponsored by a commercial firm, the gentlemen in the dark suits representing a firm of wine shippers. At that time the ship was in her post-1856 guise as shown.

The *Great Britain* in her Australian heyday, riding at anchor between the long journeys. This is the post-1856/7 version known and loved by tens of thousands of migrants.

Shipboard scenes in the latter years of the ship's working life. Members of the crew (*above*) were photographed in San Francisco in 1885. William Owen, aged 15, a stowaway on the voyage, stands in the centre of a group of three behind the wheel. The deck view (*right*) was taken in the Falkland Islands in 1886. The rails were just as they were in the Australian period and would have been held by countless excited and anxious migrants.

For more than a dozen years, the *Great Britain* enjoyed a successful, if uneventful time. This monotony was rudely interrupted on a return voyage to Liverpool in 1872 when, on 26 November, Captain John Gray disappeared. He had been ill with malaria and was alone in his cabin. When his steward went to call him, he was not there; one of the windows of his cabin was open and he had evidently fallen through it. It was apparently general knowledge that he kept money in his cabin—but it had not been taken and nothing emerged to provide any explanation at all for his disappearance.

Gray had been a popular captain, and without a doubt he stamped his personality on the Australian voyages in a quite remarkable way. The report in the *Great Britain Times* summed up what was evidently the general feeling: 'Anything he could do to promote the happiness, comfort and amusement of the passengers, he has done. His skill as a sailor and navigator, no one can doubt.'

The ship's Australian run was nearing its end. In the year of Gray's disappearance, the ship had been surveyed for Lloyd's and, in tones of polite regret, the surveyors had probably spelled the end of her life as a passenger ship: 'With all the good qualities which this ship apparently possessed, we feel an indisposition from her age of thirty years in submitting a recommendation to the committee for a classification.' To continue for long without the requisite Lloyd's classification was risky, for it made proper insurance extremely difficult. In fact, the ship completed five more voyages to Australia.

On 1 February 1876 the *Great Britain* arrived back in Liverpool after a voyage of 66 days. The homecoming was watched by a cadet on the *Theophane*, a sailing ship bound for Liverpool. Off Holyhead, he wrote, the two ships came abreast and he watched as her passengers crowded the rails, rigging and boats and 'gave us a real good cheer. The good old ship got into the Mersey one tide before us and thus ended her wonderful career as a Melbourne passenger steamer.'

Brunel's masterpiece was then laid up in Birken-
head for five years. Finally, she was put up for
auction in July 1881 by Messrs C. W. Kellock &
Company of Liverpool, whose poignant ad-
vertisement is reproduced above.

In spite of being recommended as 'admirably
adapted' for the cattle trade across the Atlantic
('She can carry livestock on three decks'), and
despite the comment of the *Liverpool Mercury*
that 'her iron is so good and strength of construction so great that with a certain outlay she
could be made a most desirable merchant ship',
the bidding reached only £6,000. For the second
time in her life, the ship was withdrawn from sale.

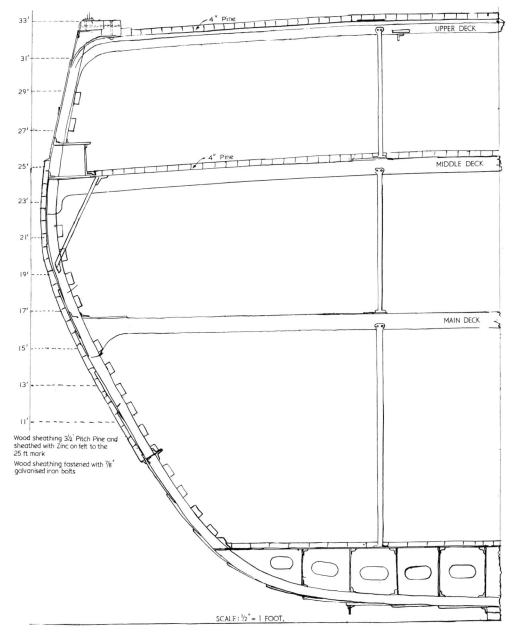

S S Great Britain

Registered dimensions : 302·6 x 51·3 x 27·5
Tonnage under deck   2683
"   gross   2735
"   nett   2640

33' 4" Pine UPPER DECK
31'
29'
27'
25' 4" Pine MIDDLE DECK
23'
21'
19'
17' MAIN DECK
15'
13'
11'

Wood sheathing 3½" Pitch Pine and
sheathed with Zinc on felt to the
25 ft mark
Wood sheathing fastened with ⅞"
galvanised iron bolts

SCALE : ½" = 1 FOOT.

In 1881 Gibbs, Bright & Company of Liverpool, the owners, were taken over by a sister company in London, Antony Gibbs & Sons. The London firm had trading connections with the west coasts of North and South America and saw a future for the ship as a cargo sailing vessel. The vessel which emerged is pictured here—the only known photograph of the *Great Britain* as a sailing ship.

Antony Gibbs saw a use for the neglected *Great Britain* and plans were made for a complete conversion to sail (see drawing on page 47). The three massive masts remained but the main mast was moved further forward to maintain the right balance with the removal of the funnel. The long deck-house, scene of so many elegant dinners beneath the great oil lights, was demolished. The engines were removed and three new cargo hatches inserted.

For some reason, possibly to protect against floating ice or as an anti-fouling measure, the hull was sheathed in pitch-pine wood from 8ft above the keel to the 25ft level, and this in turn was covered in zinc. The work was finished late in 1882 and the ship was registered on 10 November of that year. Lloyd's finally granted her the coveted A1 classification, as a cargo boat, in the 1882/3 Register.

The ship's first voyage to San Francisco began later that month, but after a few days at sea she had to turn back, leaking badly from the bolts on the wood sheathing. She sailed again on 2 December. It was not a very success-ful voyage. Neither the captain, Henry Stap, who had joined the ship only on 30 November, nor the vessel herself, appeared to enjoy the confidence of the crew. At Montevideo they refused to carry on unless the ship was lightened. Eventually 200 tons of cargo were taken off and the ship arrived in San Francisco on 2 June 1883, a voyage of 183 days. Even so, the *San Francisco*

Alta had more than a few kind words for the old ship: 'She is well worth a visit as she carries us back to Auld Lang Syne and shows conclusively that they put good work and good materials in vessels in early times.'

Her second voyage was almost as long as the first, taking over a year on the round trip. So it was not until 6 February 1886 that she set off from Cardiff on Voyage 47—her last. As the *Great Britain* neared Cape Horn, the weather became appalling with winds reaching hurricane force and waves breaking right over the ship. On 18 April the crew asked Captain Stap to put back to the Falkland Islands; he refused. For three and a half weeks the ship struggled to round Cape Horn. The cargo of coal shifted and the vessel listed dangerously for a while; then two of the top gallant masts were lost in a storm and the decks were discovered to be leaking. On 13 May, the crew once more appealed to the captain and this time, he agreed. They arrived in Stanley Harbour on 24 May 1886.

A survey was put in hand: the incredible strength of the *Great Britain* was still in evidence, for the surveyors reported 'the ship quite tight'; but the cost of repairing the masts and decks was estimated at £5,500. This was the end of her sea-going career. The expense was clearly not justified and besides, Antony Gibbs had found a willing buyer for her as she was: the Corporation of the Falkland Islands Company.

Great Britain photographed in the Falkland Islands in 1886 as she was about to begin another working life as a storehouse for wool.

Photographs have been of inestimable value to the experts now engaged in restoring the *Great Britain* to her original appearance. This view is the only known study of her stern decoration. It was taken at Port Stanley while the ship was still in her sailing ship guise, probably in the late 1890s. Visitors to the ship in Bristol today can admire the elegance of the transom and its gilt ornamentation.

The economy of the Falkland Islands has always been based on wool, and the Corporation, its major trading organisation, was looking in 1886 for a new floating wool storehouse in Port Stanley. The *Great Britain* fitted the bill perfectly and the owners were prepared to accept the modest sum of £2,000 for her. Conversion work was minimal and was conducted while the vessel lay at anchor.

For over 50 years the vessel was to ride at anchor in Port Stanley, first holding wool, then as her station in life descended further, coal. By 1888 Lloyd's Register was describing the one-time Queen of the Atlantic as a 'hulk ex-steamer'. When British warships took aboard coal before the World War I Battle of the Falklands, the *Great Britain* was the source of much of their fuel. The old ship still retained much of her magic for seafarers and she was an object of pilgrimage for the Royal Navy—as indeed she was for most people calling at the Falklands during half a century.

By 1933 the *Great Britain* was not even required as a hulk. The weather deck, by then half a century old, was beginning to leak. There were also fears that she might start to come to pieces during one of the frequent storms which hit the Falklands. If she sank, she could block the harbour of Port Stanley. Another sailing ship took her place as the port's hulk and the Falkland Islands Company wondered what it could do with its historic but apparently useless possession.

Three years later the Governor, Sir Henniker Heston, launched a fund for the vessel's preservation and restoration. It was calculated that upwards of £15,000 would be required and an appeal was made in Britain. But no response came from the public and the Admiralty called on the Atlantic Squadron to tow the ship out to sea and sink her as target practice. The Royal Navy, to its everlasting honour, declined to commit such an act and it was then decided that the vessel should be scuttled.

In April 1937 *Great Britain* was towed three miles out of Port Stanley (*right*) to the desolate Sparrow Cove, haunt of rare sea birds but few other living things. Holes were blasted in her sides to make her settle down in the mud and await a quiet future of inevitable disintegration.

Scenes of dereliction at Sparrow Cove. The lavatory pan on page 56 was one of the few items which survived many years of souvenir hunting and is now on display at the ship's museum in Bristol.

Thirty years of near total neglect followed. The ship decayed further through the war years, and there were other things for even ship lovers to think about in 1945 than the celebration of the centenary of her triumphant Atlantic début. In the immediate post-war years, too, there were so many reconstruction tasks in the world that no one thought much about the rusting hulk at the bottom of the world.

By 1960, however, people were thinking about the past again and there were the first stirrings of the feelings of conservation which are, happily, so strong today. Karl Kortum, Director of the San Francisco Maritime Museum, was one of the first to take a fresh look at the *Great Britain* about that time and he tried hard to arouse public interest in her, especially in British maritime circles.

Kortum interested William Swigert, an American businessman and engineer, in the ship and in 1967 the two men went to the Falklands to study the condition of the ironwork. Although they did not conduct a full technical examination, Kortum took a large number of photographs which proved that the ship, for all its decay, was still in one piece and worthy of fresh attention. The Americans had hopes of taking her back in some way, at some time, to San Francisco; but the ship's special significance to the British people was always a prime consideration for them. While they planned ways of getting the vessel to the US west coast, they still hoped that feelings would somehow be stirred in Britain and that the vessel would return to her proper home.

That interest eventually came, but not as a result of the activities of the American enthusiasts. Ewan Corlett, a well-known naval architect, had long been interested in the *Great Britain* and Brunel, and had been collecting references to the ship as a hobby. In November of 1967 he did what all right-thinking British men and women do when they feel strongly about a certain subject: he wrote a brief letter to *The Times* which sparked a considerable response. The text of Corlett's letter is published opposite.

FIRST IRON STEAMSHIP
From Mr. E. C. B. Corlett

Sir—The first iron-built ocean-going steamship and the first such ship to be driven entirely by a propeller was the Great Britain, designed and launched by Isambard Kingdom Brunel. This, the forefather of all modern ships, is lying a beached hulk in the Falkland Islands at this moment.

The Cutty Sark has rightly been preserved at Greenwich and H.M.S. Victory at Portsmouth. Historically the Great Britain has an equal claim to fame and yet nothing has been done to document the hulk, let alone recover it and preserve it for record.

May I make a plea that the authorities should at least document, photograph, and fully record this wreck and at best do something to recover the ship and place her on display as one of the very few really historic ships in existence.

E. C. B. Corlett
The Coach-House, Worting Park, Basingstoke, Hampshire, Nov. 8.

was little news to encourage them. Eye witness accounts considered at the meeting were generally pessimistic, and the most depressing was a report just received from the Falkland Islands Government stating that the vessel was severely corroded and doubting whether she could be towed with safety.

The official summary from the Falklands concluded: 'This report may seem unduly pessimistic but prime considerations such as expense, safety, possible disasters, must be weighed against historical interest. The writer feels the balance must be against the success of the project.'

To other men but the founders of the SS *Great Britain* Project, such an official report would have been daunting to a high degree; but they resolved to press ahead with their campaign to bring the ship home. One idea considered at that time, and advanced by the San Francisco Maritime Museum, was for the ship to be enclosed in a metal cage and then filled with polyurethane foam. That would have cost at least £1 million at the then current prices.

Corlett, however, remained optimistic. He felt that the photographic records of the Americans, and prints which he commissioned by a Port Stanley photographer, indicated that the vessel was sturdier than might appear from a casual study. In November 1968 he was given a passage from Montevideo to Port Stanley in the ice patrol ship HMS *Endurance*. With the help of Royal Navy personnel, he was able to spend five days in surveying the hulk. Corlett is pictured (*opposite page, right*) inspecting the interior of the ship and realising the ambition of half a lifetime. Corlett is on the left.

Much later the marine architect confessed that his first impression of the ship was one of depression. But as he studied the condition of the ironwork and heard the reports of naval divers, his confidence began to mount. Upon his return to London he was able to submit a fairly ebullient report to the Project. He told his colleagues that the *Great Britain* was in 'surprisingly sound overall structural condition'. And he concluded by declaring: 'The *Great Britain* is capable of salvage; the work should be within the compass of two or three months at Stanley for a salvage tug and crew, and the ship is very well worth the effort.'

But he made plain that time was not on their side. The vessel had a deep crack which was widening with time. In Corlett's own graphic report, she was 'digging her own grave'. There was not a great deal of time, perhaps five years at the very most, before she would break in two. It was therefore imperative for the Project to make its plans, and raise the necessary funds, as soon as was humanly possible.

The three paragraph letter in *The Times* provoked a warm response, first and predictably from Commander George Naish of the National Maritime Museum, Greenwich. Then came an encouraging letter from the Falkland Islands Company, and the BBC invited Dr Corlett to speak about the ship in a radio programme. Further press publicity attracted the attention of Richard Goold-Adams who was later to become Chairman of the SS *Great Britain* Project; he contacted Corlett and the two men began to discuss what might be done to save the ship.

In May 1968 a small group met in Bristol's City Museum to launch the Project. Swigert, the American, was there to give the scheme his blessing and to surrender American designs on her provided there was to be a serious British rescue attempt. But, apart from the enthusiasm of all present, there

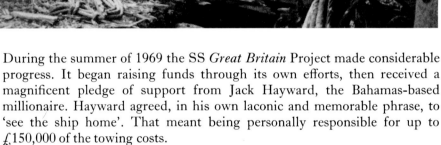

During the summer of 1969 the SS *Great Britain* Project made considerable progress. It began raising funds through its own efforts, then received a magnificent pledge of support from Jack Hayward, the Bahamas-based millionaire. Hayward agreed, in his own laconic and memorable phrase, to 'see the ship home'. That meant being personally responsible for up to £150,000 of the towing costs.

By October of that year the Project was able to announce that it was well advanced in negotiations to have the 'Crown Wreck' released to it by the Falkland Islands authorities, and that the ship's original dock (now part of the Charles Hill shipyard) could be made available for her in Bristol. It was also disclosed that a Hull-based tug company was sending a team of experts to Port Stanley to plan the great towing operation.

A happy ending to the saga seemed then to be in sight; events appeared to be working towards the desired solution. Then, in November, came a major setback. The tug company decided it could not risk becoming involved in the rescue attempt. Its experts felt the iron work was too far gone for the *Great Britain* to be made seaworthy; the risk of towing her in the open Atlantic was 'unacceptable'. The Project had to think again.

Until almost the end of 1969, Corlett and his colleagues believed that the only way the ship could come home was for her to be raised, patched up and then reinforced with buoyancy foam. In the last days of the decade, however, a remarkable new scheme was advanced by an Anglo-German company named Risdon Beazley Ulrich Harms, based in Southampton. This salvage organisation proposed that the ship be raised and then returned to Bristol on top of a large floating pontoon known as the *Mulus III*. This extraordinary craft, 250ft long and 79ft wide, would be sunk beneath the *Great Britain* in Sparrow Cove; then the ship would be lifted clean out of the water by pumping air into the sunken *Mulus*.

Corlett approved the scheme after very careful consideration, and Hayward gave it his blessing as the Project's benefactor. Within a fortnight, agreement in principle had been reached and Leslie O'Neill of the towing firm travelled to Port Stanley in January 1970 for a detailed survey. Returning to London on the 28th of that month, O'Neill said he felt the venture had an 80 per cent chance of success. That was good enough for the great adventure to begin.

Mulus III and its attendant tug *Varius II* had a salvage assignment in West Africa in the early weeks of 1970 and moved on to Montevideo when the job had been done. On Sunday 15 March the odd flotilla left Montevideo for the Falklands with Lord Strathcona representing the SS *Great Britain* Project in its finest hour. In ten days they were in Port Stanley and on 26 March work started in earnest when the pontoon was moored alongside the *Great Britain*.

The first task was to erect a temporary walkway on the rotting deck and to start patching up the holes made during the scuttling operation. The salvage team removed the masts and spars with great effort and the great crack in the ship's side was made watertight with rubber mattresses. On the 11th day, when the rough patching had been completed, pumping out of the ship began. Plugging continued as more holes were discovered; then, on the thirteenth day after the arrival of the salvage fleet, the ship came afloat unexpectedly. It was 5.30am on Tuesday 7 April 1970. After the removal of the main mast (*below left*) the vessel floated easily aboard the pontoon (*right*).

The ship was now afloat for the first time in 33 years; but, within hours of this dramatic event, a strong wind blew up and the *Great Britain* began to list in a most alarming manner. The decision was then taken, sensibly, to sink her again. So *Great Britain* was allowed to settle on the bottom of Sparrow Cove once more—and anxious ship-lovers all over the world pondered on the significance of press reports on the new 'sinking'.

The winds did not abate until Friday 10 April when the ship was successfully refloated. Now it was possible to begin the tricky task of floating her over the sunken pontoon which would then be raised to lift her out of the water. This operation was again hampered by bad weather, but by this time the ship was riding steadily on the water and giving great confidence and pleasure to all who watched her.

On 11 April the vessel was finally docked atop the pontoon. The next day, as the pontoon pushed up from beneath, the bows of the *Great Britain* came out of the water for the first time in 85 years. By the 13th, as the photographs show, she was safe and sound on the *Mulus*.

On 14 April the salvage flotilla made the short voyage to Port Stanley where the inhabitants, who for generations had thought of the ship as a permanent landmark, gave her a heart-warming welcome. Now that she was floating again, and no longer officially a 'wreck', formal ownership of the vessel was transferred from the Falkland Islands administration to the SS *Great Britain* Project.

Within ten days, after further lashing down and tidying-up, it was possible to embark upon the 7,000-mile tow home, one of the longest ever attempted in marine history. By 2 May she was in Montevideo, to receive another frenzied welcome, and to be subjected to further inspections and minor repairs in preparation for the long pull home across the Atlantic. The photograph above was taken in the Uruguayan port.

Securely moored to the pontoon, the *Great Britain* rides the Atlantic in a calmly majestic manner. The view above was taken from the towing tug *Varius II* from whose decks a watchful eye was kept on the precarious charge at all hours of the day and night. Ewan Corlett, who saw her in Montevideo, wrote years later: 'She gave an overwhelming impression to those who, like myself, had seen her deserted and dreadfully lost, alone in that far-off cove.'

The *Great Britain* left Montevideo on 6 May on the final leg of Voyage 47. On 23 June the flotilla was in Barry Roads, in sight of Penarth where the voyage started on 6 February 1886—surely the slowest sea journey in history! She had averaged only a little more than five knots on her journey home; but even this was slightly faster than the four and half knots of the outward voyage to the Falklands as a sailing ship. The next day she was in Avonmouth for a spell in dry dock and further strapping up of her hull. The photographs on this and the next two pages record her arrival in the port, a few miles from Bristol.

An eye witness account of the appearance of the *Great Britain* as she neared Avonmouth was recorded by Richard Goold-Adams who flew over the ship with Jack Hayward as the salvage flotilla passed up the Bristol Channel. For Goold-Adams the culmination of almost two years of work and organisation was 'one of the most thrilling moments of my life'.

He set down his feelings later in these words: 'I knew then that everything had been worthwhile. The *Great Britain*, truncated though she was, looked every inch a ship. Brunel's lines were as splendid as one had always supposed them to be, with a peculiar blend of dignity and beauty that had only gained from the ravages of a century and a quarter . . . If this was the hull of the world's first propeller-driven ocean liner, it was also something which had a simple grandeur of its own.'

The *Great Britain* stayed in Avonmouth for a week. Then, on 1 July 1970, she was unlocked from her pontoon. This was achieved by allowing *Mulus III* to sink beneath her in the harbour and letting the ship float on her own bottom. It was a stirring sight for all who had followed her fortunes across the world. Now she was ready for the tow up river, to re-enter the dock which had been created for her in the heart of Victorian Bristol.

68

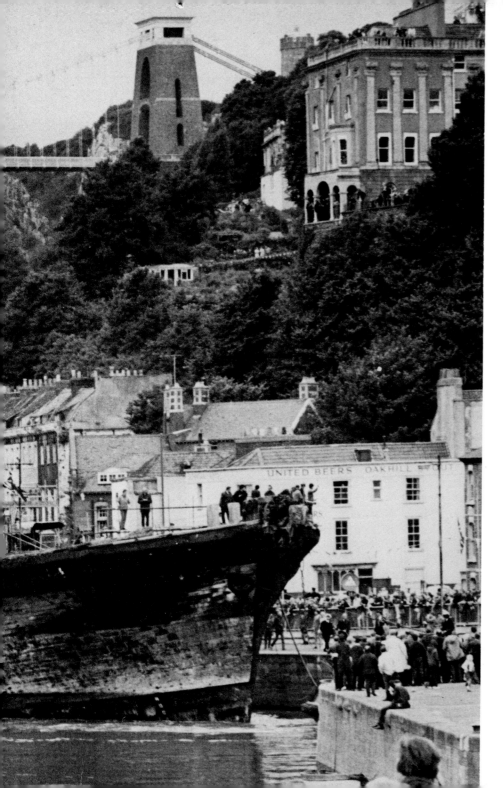

The last stage of the journey could have been the most hazardous. There was the Horseshoe Bend of the Avon to negotiate—the ship might run aground if a strong wind was blowing as she made passage through that treacherous stretch of river. Countless ships had foundered before her in the Avon and weather conditions had to be studied with great care. The Port of Bristol Authority asked the Project to insure the vessel for £1 million while she was in Avonmouth and a further £1 million for the journey to the City Docks.

By Sunday 5 July the wind, which had been gusting strongly, abated quite suddenly and the Avonmouth Harbourmaster, the river pilot and Corlett decided that the time was right for the last chapter. The tow began with a drama. Off Portishead, turning into the mouth of the river, one of the hawsers snapped. This might have been very serious but a second tow-wire held and, to the intense relief of all concerned, the ship was turned slowly up river, bound for Bristol.

The remainder of the 4-hour journey to the Floating Harbour went without a hitch. It was the ship's first passage along the Avon since 11 December 1844. When she first went to sea, Brunel's famous suspension bridge had not been completed; now the bridge was a revered landmark in the city, crowded with spectators and traffic. She had left a Britain on the verge of becoming the mightiest maritime and industrial power in the history of the world; she was returning to a nation with decimated naval and merchant fleets and racked by economic and political crises.

More than 100,000 people crowded every vantage point along the Avon to cheer the old lady home. Large numbers of them had slept in their cars overnight to gain prime positions. By general consent, it was the most spontaneous and heartfelt demonstration Bristol had ever seen. No one who was beside the Avon that day will ever forget the sight of the ship, negotiating first the celebrated Horseshoe Bend, then passing under the Brunel bridge. The excitement did not end until the ship had been turned round in the wide harbour by the City Centre and moored, like any other commercial craft, at Y Wharf in Canons Marsh.

71

When the *Great Britain* was pulled into the Floating Harbour on that sunny July day she won the affection of every Bristolian, and gave members of the Project confidence that her future in the city was assured. Until then, official reaction to the ship had been cautious, even hostile in some quarters. There were City Councillors on both sides of the political fence who were dubious about allowing the ship into the port, extraordinary though such a view seems today with the ship established as a premier tourist attraction.

One reason was the fact that, at the end of the 1960s, the city was preparing to close the inner port area to commercial shipping and there were fears that the presence of the *Great Britain* might interfere with major long-term development plans. There was also the suspicion that the Project could be looking to the council for strong financial support so that the ship might become a permanent burden on the rates. And, when the tow home became a reality, there was apprehension that the old ship might sink in Avonmouth or the river and block the shipping lanes.

In addition to all these local suspicions, there was the fact that the rescue of the ship from the Falklands had been conceived and carried through by private individuals who lived, and worked, outside the city. Bristolians are proud and clannish and years were to pass before the SS *Great Britain* Project became fully accepted into the rich fabric of Bristol life. Now the Project has its own local committee and fund-raising efforts; in 1970 the private enthusiasts involved were working from London.

The latter part of 1970 and all of 1971 was occupied with inconclusive discussions with the Council about the ship's future. Although the Brunel dock was felt by the Project to be the most appropriate resting place, alternative ideas had to be considered in view of the official reluctance to confirm the ship's future place in the dock area. The most significant of these was a scheme to tow the vessel to London and place her on a pontoon beside the new St Katherine's Dock development on the Thames. Such a site could have attracted more visitors and generated far greater funds for restoration work. A detailed plan was prepared, and an artist's impression is given on page 78; but the idea was finally abandoned at an historic meeting of the Project on 25 January 1972.

The Project then announced that it would keep the *Great Britain* in Bristol and would do all in its power to see that she remained there in the historic Great Western Dock. The Project would take no part in discussions with anyone to consider other sites unless and until its Bristol aims proved finally to be unattainable. So she was home, forever.

A Queen's Consort had launched the *Great Britain;* it was appropriate that Prince Philip should fulfil a similar role when the ship was returned to her dock 127 years later. And, by an extraordinary coincidence, the highest tide of the month—necessary to see the vessel comfortably into the Great Western Dock—was the evening of 19 July. This, it will be remembered, was the date on which the *Great Western* had been launched in 1837, the laying of the first plate of the *Great Britain* in 1839 and the launching of the same ship.

All these historical coincidences augured well for a successful re-entry and the optimists were proved right. Weather conditions were perfect, the tide was better than predicted and the ship was redocked smoothly—despite the fact that there was only 6in clearance on each side and under the keel.

Prince Philip, standing on the deck, was a fascinated spectator of the inch-by-inch docking operation. As a former Royal Navy officer, he was particularly impressed by the way the vessel was positioned precisely above the keel blocks on which she would rest once the water had been pumped from the dock. There was no doubt that the keel blocks were 'ship-shape and Bristol fashion': they were the same blocks that had borne her until 1843.

This was the extraordinary appearance the *Great Britain* presented to the world in her early weeks in the dock. The wooden cladding, dating from her sailing ship days, had first to be removed together with hundreds of tons of mud, scale and rotting marine life. Cleaning of the ironwork then began.

High-pressure water jets were used for the operation as this was judged to be least likely to damage the fabric of the vessel. The task took more than two years to complete, and pieces of the cladding found their way into thousands of British homes as souvenirs of the ship.

Fragile ironwork discovered during the cleaning was restored to its original thickness by patching with specially prepared, tough glass fibre. Ten thousand bolt holes were filled with iron bolts made to look like the original rivet heads. The most exciting part of the early restoration work was the opening up again of the portholes which revealed something of how she had appeared to the world in the 1840s.

Prince Philip has always taken a keen interest in the restoration of the *Great Britain*. He is seen here inspecting the ship soon after its arrival in 1970 and discussing with members of the Project the immense task which lay ahead. He is pictured with Richard Goold-Adams on his left (Chairman of the Project), Ewan Corlett (naval architect), Jack Hayward (the Project's great benefactor), and Lord Strathcona, who was present at the refloating. More views of the scene which greeted the party are shown on the following pages.

One of the earliest decisions of the SS *Great Britain* Project was that the ship should be restored to her 1845 condition, the elegant six-masted version depicted with loving care (*below*) in this modern painting by Keith Griffin. But a vast amount of money and years of effort would be necessary to transform her from the hulk that quickly became a Bristol landmark in the early 1970s. At first it seemed that ten years would suffice; but after a decade it was clear that 1985 was a more realistic target for full restoration.

The Project could only obtain the necessary funds through donations, in cash and kind, by admission charges to visitors at the dock, and through sales at a souvenir shop established beside the ship. Happily, the immense public interest in the vessel brought a reasonable cash flow from the outset. Over 200,000 people paid to see her in the first year; by the fourth anniversary of her return, the half million total had been reached; and it took a further five years to double that figure. By the tenth anniversary of the *Great Britain*'s return, in July 1980, attendances had topped 1,250,000.

In her first decade in the dock, the Project spent more than £500,000 on restoration and maintenance. A further large sum was represented by donations of materials and services of 600 British companies. At the end of 1980, the Project's Council estimated that upwards of £800,000 in donations and income would be required for the five years to the close of 1985, by which time she should be in the state that so gratified Queen Victoria 140 years earlier.

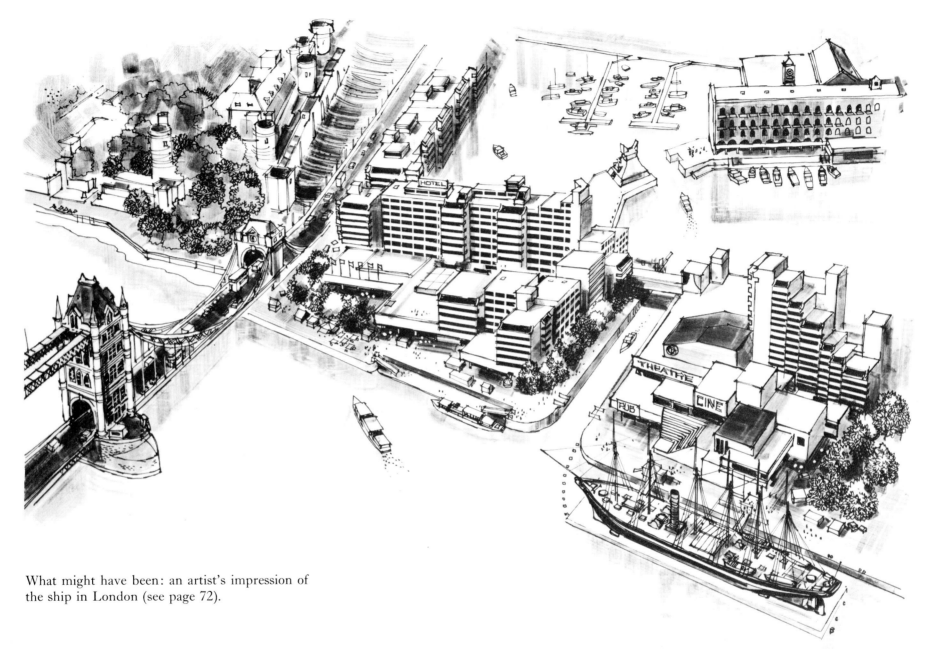

What might have been: an artist's impression of
the ship in London (see page 72).

SS Great Britain at Tower Bridge

Items presented to the *Great Britain* Museum have ranged from a ship's biscuit to the captain's bath (*right*). The Champagne label (*bottom left*) is a rare relic of one of the early transatlantic voyages. In 1978 bottles of Mumm Champagne bearing a replica of this label were sold to raise funds for the ship's restoration at Bristol's World Wine Fair.

In the decade or more since the ship came home, an unusual museum has been built up at the dockside, largely based upon gifts from members of the public. Among the most interesting are copies of ship's newspapers produced during the long voyages to and from Australia. Left with plenty of time on their hands, passengers would get together to produce fascinating accounts of shipboard life which were then printed formally at the end of each passage. Among publications which survive are *The Cabinet* (1861), the *Great Britain Magazine or Weekly Screw* (1862) and the *SS Great Britain Times* of 1865.

These newspapers, along with several passengers' diaries which have survived, provide a great deal of information on what life was actually like on board. The newspapers, inevitably, give only a partial view for it was the saloon (first-class) passengers who in the main organised and wrote the papers, and whose home-made entertainments featured in their columns. For first hand information on the other classes we have to rely more on private diaries, journals and letters. Nevertheless, the newspapers give a vivid and immediate glimpse of the Victorian middle class at their enforced leisure which is also curiously touching.

Two main problems must have dogged the passengers: boredom and overcrowding. Even for those travelling first class on a ship as relatively spacious as the *Great Britain*, they were faced with two months of little to do, and precious little space in which to do it. They set about alleviating these problems with energy. The aim of the *Great Britain Times* was confidently stated in its first editorial: 'It is the duty of every rational man to enhance as far as he is able the happiness of those around him, and the originators, being convinced of the truth of this, convened a meeting . . . and finally decided on having a newspaper weekly issued.'

This plan was duly carried out, and the *Great Britain Times* appeared each week, with its avowed intention of causing 'Amusement to All—Offence to None', and contained reports of the concerts, plays and recitals organised by the saloon passengers. Extracts from the log and a daily progress report were included for the information of its readers and they were, presumably, diverted and entertained by the jokes, the poems, ballads and social diaries that completed each issue.

On Sundays, however, dancing properly gave way to more serious activities, and services were held for the Anglicans, Roman Catholics and Presbyterians among the passengers. A Sunday School was also organised.

The ship's barometer, now on display in the museum, was doubtless the subject of daily comment as the *Great Britain* steamed across the world. The chair was almost certainly used in the luncheon which followed the launching ceremony in 1845.

Concerts were a weekly feature of this particular voyage. In the first week, a 'Grand Concert' took place in the saloon quarters which started with an overture played on the piano by 'Miss Russell and Mr Anderson, which was tastefully played and duly appreciated by the large audience . . . Mrs Cookworthy, *prima donna* of the evening, then gave "Sing, Birdie, Sing" very effectually and sweetly.' Two weeks later, an 'IMMENSE ATTRACTION' was advertised in the *Times*: the 'favourite Petite Comedy in two Acts, entitled "Perfection or The Lady of Munster"', which in the eyes of its captive audience was also, evidently, a great success.

The voyage even gave rise to its own piece of music: the 'Great Britain Galop' was composed on board and was judged to be 'sure of many new admirers and a ready sale'. Unfortunately, it does not appear to have survived.

During the warmer weather, dancing on deck under lamps strung from the rigging became the main diversion. Captain Gray himself would lead the dancing, and this activity even received a qualified nod of approval from the upright editors of the *Times*: of course, it could be 'misused and perverted' but, they argued, 'if persons are capable of being corrupted by dancing, they will find some much more effective mode of being so'.

THE "GREAT BRITAIN" TIMES,

PUBLISHED EXPRESSLY FOR THE PASSENGERS OF THE S.S. "GREAT BRITAIN,"

AND CONTAINING

AMUSEMENT TO ALL—OFFENCE TO NONE!

No. 3. *'I'Sea,' Saturday, November 11th, 1865.* GRATIS.

ADVERTISEMENTS.

PAPER! PAPER!

FOR THE "GREAT BRITAIN TIMES."

The Editor of this paper is run short of the wherewithal to carry on the "Times." He will, therefore, feel thankful if his numerous friends will either dispose to him. letter or foolscap paper, at a low rate, or present him with the same FREE GRATIS FOR NOTHING, as it suits their convenience. The gift, however, will be preferred. The same left at No. 17, Collins Street, will be duly received by our porter.

AMUSEMENTS.

THE ROYAL SALOON THEATRE.

This favourite House will shortly open with A POWERFUL COMPANY in a piece of great interest. Further particulars in future advertisements. Nov. 10th, 1865.

WANTED, very urgently for the lost heart advertised for in first issue, now found—the Sacred Rites of Matrimony. Address, stating fees, "Heart," Times office.

LOST, on the 9th instant, our Editor's equilibrium. Whoever finds the same and returns it to the owner in a wheelbarrow, will be liberally rewarded with a glass of h-ale without water.

THE "GREAT BRITAIN" MUSIC HALL.

ANOTHER

GRAND CONCERT

will be given in this place, weather permitting, on Thursday Evening, the 16th inst., performance to commence at 8 p.m.

PROGRAMME.

PART FIRST.

Duet .. .. Wedding Waltz,—Piano. ... Miss Russell & Mr. Anderson.
Solo & Chorus "Let me Kiss him for his Mother." Mrs. Cookworthy, Misses Russell, Adams, and Marr, Messrs. Anderson, Venables, and Cookworthy.
Song .. ... Lo Squarto .. .. Mrs. Cookworthy.
Song .. ... Sargo al Factotum .. .. Mr. Venables.
Song .. .. Spirit Song .. .. Miss Adams.

PART SECOND.

Duet Qui Viva, (Galop)—Piano .. Misses Russell & Adams.
Solo & Chorus "Hazel Dell." Mrs. Cookworthy, Misses Russell, Adams, and Marr, Messrs. Cookworthy, Anderson and Venables.
Song .. .. "Bolero." .. .. Mrs Cookworthy.
Song .. "Old Simon the Cellarer." .. Mr. Venables.
Song .. "Autumn Fruits." .. .. Mr. Anderson.

"GOD SAVE THE QUEEN."

NOTICE TO CORRESPONDENTS.

Permit us to remind you that two o'clock p.m. of every Thursday, is the latest time we can accept contributions.

Pleeceman X. Your ballad is with thanks declined.

A Looker on. Your Sporting News is respectfully declined.

A Passenger. Owing *to a press of matter*, we cannot insert your note; the captain will, however, see that no smoking is allowed 'tween decks."

When communications verge too far in personality, we are bound to reject them.

Divine Services will be held in the Saloon, in the Second Cabin, and in the Intermediate, on Sunday next (to-morrow). All are invited.

The "Great Britain" Times,

PUBLISHED WEEKLY.

Life on board ship is indeed very monotonous, and anything therefore got up for the sake of amusement and to render the time more lightsome and agreeable meets with due appreciation. It is, however, taken for granted that such amusement will tend chiefly for our intellectual and harmless enjoyment than for any mischievous intent. It is not to be expected that mortals are to pass their life on land in unceaseless labour without appropriating occasionally a portion of time to the varied amusements of life, nor do we think the voyager should allow his time to pass altogether idly away without devising some means to amuse himself betimes. We maintain that this spirit of recreation forms more or less an essential part of our existence, and that it materially benefits our health and strengthens our limbs. Without amusement on board, life would be to the weary passenger a drudgery and a burden; with it, and we take pride in stating that we have a little, everything appears in a pleasant aspect, and our disagreeables are unfelt in the enjoyments we possess. Amusements may be either of an intellectual and harmless nature, or of an offensive and injurious tendency. The mind, as well as the physical powers of man requires exercise, otherwise they will prove of little value to the possessor, and there being no reason why these should not be taken care of and cultivated, in order that they may be of use to those around them, we ask everyone to bestir themselves in this matter. Anxious to promote amusement, and desirous of seeing everyone enjoying themselves, we here offer a few suggestions, which we think if acted upon in a proper manner, will assist in making our time to pass more pleasantly away. Music may justly be regarded as an innocent and delightful amusement, and has the advantage of being social as well as solitary. It can be made to produce a sense of high moral feeling, and it also may be made to produce feelings of an opposite character, which especially on board ship, is too often indulged in, but which we trust our readers will do their best to repress. Every one can either join in or enjoy this amusement, and we are certain that in this little world of ours a sufficient number can be raised to have concerts weekly, or as often as is convenient. Music no doubt was given to us for our amusement and it is our duty to take it in that light, and to feel thankful for it. Lectures upon subjects of interest would form another kind of amusement, which we think would not be amiss on board the "Great Britain." If such did not exceed half an hour in delivery, two or three parties could hold forth on the same night. There are several gentlemen on board quite able to gratify us in this way, and who could at the same time form a discussion class, and thus cause a still greater attraction. We commend dancing also as a very good amusement. This of course, just like everything else, may be misused and perverted, but it can also be made an innocent, and healthy accomplishment. Possibly it is considered frivolous and corrupting, but we hold that if persons are capable of being corrupted by dancing, they will find some much more effective mode of becoming so, if this was denied to them. We believe there are enough of musical instruments on board, together with parties who will be only too glad to discourse lively tunes for the benefit of those who now and then wish to trip it on the light fantastic toe! Other amusements might be mentioned in which during the week we could engage ourselves, but our limited space prevents us from entering into their detail. We are however satisfied that if those we have mentioned are carried on vigorously, and with every brotherly feeling, they will be sufficient to pass agreeably many of our leisure hours. In another column will be found the report of the Intermediate Concert, which took place last Thursday evening. We understand it is the intention of the Intermediate Minstrels to have such meetings repeatedly. The progress which our ship has made according to our Captain's letter, since our last issue, is very satisfactory and encouraging. Besides, the general health of all on board continuing good, gives us much cause for thankfulness.

THE "GREAT BRITAIN" TIMES,

PUBLISHED EXPRESSLY FOR THE PASSENGERS OF THE S.S. "GREAT BRITAIN."

AND CONTAINING

AMUSEMENT TO ALL—OFFENCE TO NONE!

No. 6. *'I'Sea,' Saturday, December 2nd, 1865.* GRATIS.

ADVERTISEMENTS.

THEATRE ROYAL.

Sole Lessee and Manager....... CAPT. COOKWORTHY.
Conductor of Orchestra.......... J. H. ANDERSON, ESQ.

IMMENSE ATTRACTION

JONES IS COMING!!!

Engagement for one night only of SAMUEL BRIGHT!!
Weather permitting. this Theatre will shortly re-open for the final performance of the season, when the favourite plays of
"JOHN DOBBS," and "COOL AS A CUCUMBER"
Will be performed, with other Entertainments.—For further particulars, see Hand Bills.—Children with their parents unadmitted.

FOUND in front of the door of the Captain's State Room, a white handled pen-knife. The Owner may have it on proving property and paying expenses, at the office of this paper.

WANTED, about nine o'clock every evening, for several 'tween deck passengers, a quantity of gruel. Apply to Dr. Mc Donald, F.R.S., G. B., Steambridge Street, G. B.

PASSENGERS' Linen carefully washed and punctually returned. Terms reasonable. Address Washaway, "Times" Office. 2nd December, 1865.

WANTED for the Editor's box, a few pithy, racy, and brief articles on Love at Sea.

NOTICES TO CORRESPONDENTS.

"Bachelor." We decline inserting your contribution, as they seem uninteresting.

"One perplexed." The information you want, will be given next week.

DIVINE SERVICES.—It is understood that these Services will be held on deck on Sunday next, as follows.—
In the morning (Church of England), at 10-30.
" (Roman Catholic) "
In the Evening (Presbyterian) 6 o'clock.

The "Great Britain" Times,

PUBLISHED WEEKLY.

CAPTAIN GRAY.

The re-appearance of our esteemed commander on deck on Thursday last (after a week's severe indisposition) was the cause of general satisfaction and gladness to all on board. He appeared very much reduced with the sickness—we sincerely hope that in a few days he will regain his wonted health and vigor, and be able to undertake his onerous duties.

The manner in which his return was greeted evidently testified the great respect in which he was held by all. He has without doubt won the affections of all—not only for the care and attention he has during the voyage shown to his duties—but for the uniform courtesy and kindness we have received from him, as well as for the unwearied solicitude by day and night for his furtherance of our happiness and security.

It is very evident, from the fact of the Second Cabin and Intermediate copies of our last publication having been either thrown overboard, or otherwise destroyed, that there are several parties on board who are extremely anxious to crush our humble periodical, and frustrate the object we have in view, viz..—of affording amusement. We cannot exactly state who these parties are, but we believe our suspicions against a few belonging respectively to the Second Cabin, Intermediate, and Steerage are correct, but we refrain from mentioning names. Whoever they are we can assure them that their attempts to hurt us are vain, and that their conduct—childish as it is—not to us alone, but to the general public, will like "illwishes return to their own bosom." Despite every such dastardly attempt, we will continue to publish as before, feeling perfectly satisfied that we have the respect of the majority, and their encouragement to "press on."

On account of this our committee, in order to secure the copies published, have determined to place the copies in the hands of Messrs. Bantock and Jackson, who will, after seeing the same publicly read at the various cabins at the time formerly agreed to, return them to the editor.

LOCAL NEWS.

FATAL ACCIDENT.—In the latter part of last week a fatal accident occurred to a youth about six years of age, by name Charles Wortman, the mother of whom is one of the steerage passengers and its father a resident of Victoria. It would appear that the child was led from curiosity to approach the aperture, through which the windsail passes to convey the cold air to the Engineers, &c., below, when suddenly slipping fell through the hole on to the engine, about 21 feet below his head coming in contact with one of the cylinders. One of the engineers being close at hand immediately dragged the child from its perilous position, when surgical assistance was speedily rendered, but all to no purpose, as life was quite extinct in a few minutes after the accident happened. The body was committed to the deep at 6 p.m. on the 24th, amidst deep regrets.

On Sabbath last Divine Services were held on deck. The Meeting were very numerously attended At 10-30 Dr. Newbold read the Church of England Service. At the same hour, and at another quarter of the deck, a Roman Catholic Service was held by Rev. Mr. Ford. In the afternoon several ladies belonging to the saloon collected together several children and spent an interesting hour in Sabbath School lessons. In the evening Presbyterian Service was held. Mr. Ritchie gave a discourse from Ecclesiastes, 9 chapter, 10 verse, and the Rev. Mr. Parker opened and closed the meeting. The reverend gentlemen expressed his regret that the state of his health prevented him from having service oftener, and intimated that he would endeavour to preach next Lord's day.

On Monday Evening last several of our seamen spent an hour or two singing songs. The numerous spectators testified their appreciation of the excellent music, by frequent loud applause and cheers.

Some beautiful sun sets were seen during the week.

Several evenings were pleasantly passed by the passengers in dancing to the sweet music of Mr. Jackson, whose disinterested services to promote harmony cannot be too highly prized.

"WELCOME, LITTLE STRANGER."

We have the pleasure to record the first birth which has taken place during our voyage. This important event took place yesterday. The parents' name is "Wycherly," and belong to the intermediate. We believe the object is a female child. The arrival of this stranger was heartily welcomed by all, and being of a peculiar race which cannot boast of having any fatherland and no country, it is looked upon as a "wonder of the age."

THE "GREAT BRITAIN" TIMES,

PUBLISHED EXPRESSLY FOR THE PASSENGERS OF THE S.S. "GREAT BRITAIN,"

AND CONTAINING

AMUSEMENT TO ALL—OFFENCE TO NONE!

GRATIS.

To avoid imposition, notices of Births, Marriages, and Deaths must be *previously* authenticated by a responsible comical personage, to secure their insertion herein. The following have been duly authenticated, and we take pleasure in inserting them.

BIRTHS.

TIMES. On board, on the morning of this day, the first publication of the "Great Britain" Times. Great Rejoicing!

MARRIAGES.

RITCHIE. Within the inside of a certain saloon on board the S.S. "Great Britain," on her passage from Melbourne towards Liverpool, G. Ritchie, Esq., of Auckland, to Miss—— to be, perhaps continued. No cards.

DEATHS.

DYED. Suddenly at the barbarous establishment of a hair cutter, in the third cabin, in the prime of life, on the 27th inst., a Pair of Whiskers, much and justly lamented. Friends will please accept of this intimation.

CONUNDRUMS.—We wish our readers to send us answers to the following :—

1.—Why is Commander Gray like a certain great Statesman?

2.—Why should Captain Gray marry the Queen of England?

ANSWERS TO LAST.

1. Because he has won a name for the "Great Britain," and always steered her clear of opposing obstacles.

2. Because he is always anxious to return quick to his Victoria.

CRINOLINES.—Ladies are requested to take care how they use this garment. On Wednesday last, as one of the fair sex was arranging to sit down to dine in one of the cabins of the vessel, her crinoline swept the handsome round of roast beef off the table. Whether the intention was to make away with it, we will not say, but we confess it would have been a hard task, as the overlookers were numerous, watchful, and hungry.

"OH ITS HARD TO DIE FRAE' HAME.

It is with sorrow we record the death of a Mr. Barber, a second class passenger, on Monday last, the 23rd inst., of consumption. The deceased, we believe, belonged to Shefford, Bedfordshire, and had about eighteen months ago left England for the colonies, and had during that time visited Auckland, Brisbane, Sydney and Melbourne. The change, however, apparently made him worse instead of better. We understand he took his passage in this vessel with the view of reaching home as speedily as possible in order to—before his removal, which he knew was fast approaching,—to have a look at his affectionate father, his only parent. This shows the frailty of humanity. Our fondest hopes, our best expectations, may in a moment be alike taken away. This should act as a warning to each of us to be ready, knowing not what a day or an hour may bring forth. The brief period Mr. Barber has been with us, causes us to mourn him more, for the little we saw of him showed us that he was not only of a quiet and pious disposition, but that he was preparing for the great change. We unite with his absent relatives in their grief, hoping that the fatherly hand of Providence will comfort and console them in this their hour of trial.

THE "GREAT BRITAIN" MUSIC HALL.

A GRAND CONCERT

will be given in this Hall on Friday, the 3rd proximo, commence at 8 p.m. precisely.

PROGRAMME.

PART FIRST.

Overture .. Piano-Forte .. Miss Russell and Mr. Anderson.

Quartette .. "Come Where my Love Lies Dreaming."
   Mrs. Cookworthy, Miss Adams and Messrs. Cookworthy and Venables.

Song .. .. "Sing, Birdie, Sing" .. .. Mrs. Cookworthy.

Song .. .. "Good Rhein Wine" .. .. Mr. Venables.

Duet .. "Tel Rammento" Mrs. Cookworthy & Miss Adams.

PART SECOND.

Duet .. "Piano-Forte Semiramide" .. Miss Russell

Trio .. "Hark, 'tis the Indian Drum" .. Miss Adams,
   Messrs. Cookworthy and Venables.

Song .. "Una Voce Poca Fa" .. Mrs. Cookworthy.

Song .. "As I View those Scenes so Charming" Miss Adams.

Song .. "Friend of the Brave" .. Mr. Venables.

"GOD SAVE THE QUEEN."

Tickets free—to be had Everywhere.

The Cabinet, a 'Repository of Facts, Figures and Fancies', dates from an earlier voyage, this time out to Australia, which took place in 1861. The *Great Britain* played a remarkable role in the migrant traffic and it has been estimated that a quarter of a million present-day Australians are descended from people who travelled in the ship during two momentous decades.

The cause of the massive migration was, of course, gold. Discovered in Victoria in the early 1850s, it transformed the colony. By 1861, the year of *The Cabinet*, Melbourne was a city of 120,000 inhabitants with at least three good theatres, 'noble buildings' and 'fine, wide streets'.

The voyage that *The Cabinet* records was a distinguished one, for among the passengers were the Eleven of All England, the first English cricket team to visit Australia, a fact proudly announced on the cover. Lectures, dancing and concerts were among the entertainments organised on the voyage. The cricketers paced the decks and played quoits to make up for the lack of practice facilities, no doubt pondering on their duty, as *The Cabinet* put it, 'to maintain the honour of England in the cricket field'.

One of the facts that emerges from these records is that the occupation of ordinary seamen in those days was a dangerous one. Many of the newspapers and diaries contain reports of sailors falling off masts or overboard. A passenger writing in 1900 and recalling his trip on the *Great Britain* in 1859 described an incident which must have presented Captain Gray with an appalling decision:

> South of the Equator a sailor was washed off the forecastle Bowsprit yard arm. A life buoy was promptly thrown at him, which he seized hold of. We (were) going full before the wind at great speed . . . The second mate and willing helpers stood ready, their eyes fixed on the skipper, waiting his decision—he looks up at the sails, out upon the boisterous waves, and at his men and decides 'No! I dare not let you go—your lives would all be sacrificed before I could bring the ship about and pick you up again.'

The passengers, the diarist recounted, raised £60 for the sailor's widow.

One of the biggest problems facing the stewards and storekeepers of the ship on the Australian run was the provision of food. With up to 700 passengers and 140 crew on board for more than two months, the quantities required were enormous. Yet they were able to offer a remarkable variety of fare, as the modern reconstruction (*right*) of a typical day's menu shows.

The ship's accommodation included a 'cow house' and space for 160 sheep, 40 pigs and 1,200 poultry. The cow provided fresh milk for saloon passengers; in the second cabin, preserved milk was the order of the day. The intermediate and steerage passengers had none provided and so would often bring supplies of their own. Fresh water, incidentally, was provided by two condensers which were capable of distilling about 1,500 gallons a day.

By having live animals on board, the problem of providing fresh food was, of course, partly solved. This, however, necessitated yet further stores: *The Cabinet* in 1861 lists 4 tons of hay, 2 tons of mangold wurzel and 120 bushels of grain among its stores of animal feed.

For the first-class passengers, the provisions were evidently extremely good, and a large part of their day must have been spent in the dining room, with breakfast at 9.00am, lunch at midday, dinner at 4.00pm and tea at 7.30pm. First-class passengers were waited on, and with a full passenger list this must sometimes have resulted in rather long drawn out meals. One of the saloon travellers described the first meal on board ship thus:

Friday dinner I can never forget, first remove—soup—then a succession of removes—waiters taking away each one's plate, as soon as finished, at the expiration of an hour or so we

SS Great Britain

MENU

JULY 6th, 1861

DINNER—SALOON

Soup
Vermicilli

Dishes
1 Saddle Mutton, Jelly Sauce
4 Roast Mutton, Baked Potatoes
3 Roast Pork, Apple Sauce
2 Roast Geese, Apple Sauce
2 Roast Veal and Bacon
2 Roast Ducks
2 Roast Fowls
3 Boiled Mutton, Caper Sauce
2 Boiled Fowls
2 Braised Mutton
2 Braised Fowls, Mushroom Sauce
2 Stewed Ducks and Olives
1 Forced Turkey, Mint Sauce

1 Chevaux de Frize Lamb
1 Corned Beef
1 Corned Pork
1 Corned Ham
1 Corned Tongue
3 Mutton Cutlets
3 Braised Cutlets
3 Curried Fowl
3 Chicken and Ham Pies
6 Green Peas
6 French Beans
8 Boiled Potatoes
8 Mashed Potatoes
6 Boiled Rice

Pastry
6 Plum Puddings

6 Rice Puddings
6 Batter Puddings
6 Custard Puddings
3 Gooseberry Tarts
3 Blackcurrant Tarts
6 Open Jam Tarts
6 Omelettes
6 Macaroni and Cheese

Dessert
6 Oranges
6 Preserved Ginger
6 Raisins
6 Almonds
6 Walnuts
6 Barcelona Nuts

DINNER—SECOND CABIN

Soup
Mutton

Dishes
2 Roast Pork, Apple Sauce
5 Roast Mutton
4 Boiled Mutton, Caper Sauce
11 Fresh Potatoes
11 Boiled Rice

Pastry
7 Plum Puddings
7 Fruit Tarts
7 Rice Puddings

DINNER—3rd CABIN AND STEERAGE

Preserved Meat   Plum Pudding

"GREAT BRITAIN" STEAM CLIPPER.

67th Dinner August 2nd 1861

BILL OF FARE.

Dishes.		Roast.	Boiled.	Dishes.	VEGETABLES, ASSORTED.
	Pea Soup				
	Salmon Fish	1	6		Pastry. *Tartlets*
3	*Pork Apple Sauce*		6		Plum Pudding.
	Beef.... *Corned*		6		Rice do.
1	Mutton....				Suet do.
2	Veal.... *Curried* 3 *Mutton*				Bread and Butter Pudding.
	Turkeys....				Roll do.
	Geese .... *Apple Sauce*				Custard *Calves*
1	Ducks....	1	6		College do.
3	Fowls....	2 1			Apple do.
	Chickens				Apple Tarts.
6	Mutton Cutlets....				Fruit do.
	Veal do. *Roast*				Open do.
	Stewed Steaks				Omelettes.
	Fricassee of Fowl....				Maccaroni.
6	Currie.... *Vol au Vent Lobster*				French Pastry.
	Tripe....				Stewed Prunes.
1	Ham....				
1	Tongue				**DESSERT.**
1	Pork....				*Figs Raisins*
	Mutton Pies....				*Almond Walnuts*
1	Pigs' Head....				*Bar Nuts*
	Haricot				

had little relish for any thing—and when the second course and dessert came round it was somewhere about two hours or more.

At any rate, the surroundings were pleasant: the saloon was a 'beautiful, lighted apartment', lined with mirrors and the seats covered in crimson velvet and 'everything that luxury could invent to make the meal agreeable'. The achievement of the stewards can be seen from a splendid 'Bill of Fare' which has survived from 1861 and is reproduced at left. What is most remarkable about this particular menu is that it appeared 67 days after the vessel had left Liverpool and within 2 days of the completion of the voyage.

The other classes did not, naturally, fare as well as those in the saloon. It seems they had to organise their own meals, collecting their food from the baker's shop and the butcher's shop themselves, and washing up afterwards. In 1875, an Irish emigrant travelling to Australia kept a diary of his journey, and a good part of it was concerned with food:

Monday 6th September. Our breakfast was none of the best today—nearly impossible to break the biscuit and if it had not been for the butter I had it would have been wasted. I made a blunder today in not attending at the butcher's shop for my pork so we had only Peasoup and Preserved Potatoes for dinner.

Tuesday 7th September. I got a few lbs. Bacon at 1/6 per lb and a 3lb loaf for 1/6; it is a fearful price but the biscuit is too hard.

Friday 24th September. Today I am messman again and miss my beef having to go for a loaf and there was such a crush at the store I had to wait till after 10 o'clock and then the butcher had shut up, rather a bad beginning for mess.

The ship's bell (*right*) is now preserved in Bristol.

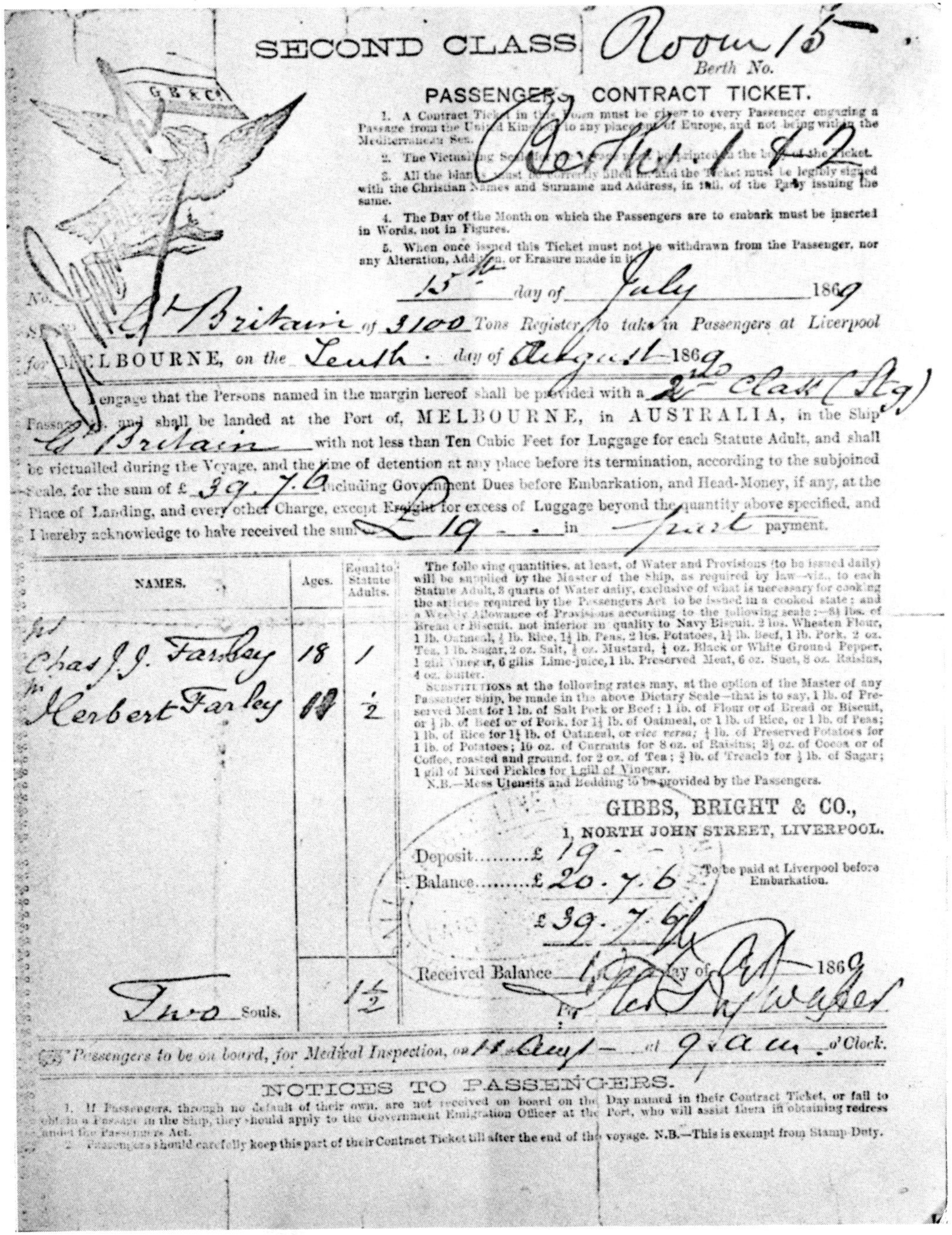
SECOND CLASS Room 15

Berth No.

PASSENGERS' CONTRACT TICKET.

1. A Contract Ticket in this Form must be given to every Passenger engaging a Passage from the United Kingdom to any place out of Europe, and not being within the Mediterranean Sea.

2. The Victualling Scale must be printed in the body of the Ticket.

3. All the blanks must be correctly filled in and the Ticket must be legibly signed with the Christian Names and Surname and Address, in full, of the Party issuing the same.

4. The Day of the Month on which the Passengers are to embark must be inserted in Words, not in Figures.

5. When once issued this Ticket must not be withdrawn from the Passenger, nor any Alteration, Addition, or Erasure made in it.

Berth 1 & 2

15th day of July 1869

G^t Britain of 3100 Tons Register, to take in Passengers at Liverpool for MELBOURNE, on the Tenth day of August 1869

I engage that the Persons named in the margin hereof shall be provided with a 2^d Class (Stg) Passage, and shall be landed at the Port of, MELBOURNE, in AUSTRALIA, in the Ship G^t Britain with not less than Ten Cubic Feet for Luggage for each Statute Adult, and shall be victualled during the Voyage, and the time of detention at any place before its termination, according to the subjoined Scale, for the sum of £ 39. 7. 6 including Government Dues before Embarkation, and Head-Money, if any, at the Place of Landing, and every other Charge, except Freight for excess of Luggage beyond the quantity above specified, and I hereby acknowledge to have received the sum of £ 19 . . in part payment.

NAMES.	Ages.	Equal to Statute Adults.
Chas J. J. Farley	18	1
Herbert Farley	11	½
Two Souls.		1½

The following quantities, at least, of Water and Provisions (to be issued daily) will be supplied by the Master of the Ship, as required by law—viz., to each Statute Adult, 3 quarts of Water daily, exclusive of what is necessary for cooking the articles required by the Passengers Act to be issued in a cooked state; and a Weekly Allowance of Provisions according to the following scale:—3½ lbs. of Bread or Biscuit, not inferior in quality to Navy Biscuit, 2 lbs. Wheaten Flour, 1 lb. Oatmeal, ½ lb. Rice, 1½ lb. Peas, 2 lbs. Potatoes, 1¼ lb. Beef, 1 lb. Pork, 2 oz. Tea, 1 lb. Sugar, 2 oz. Salt, ½ oz. Mustard, ¼ oz. Black or White Ground Pepper, 1 gill Vinegar, 6 gills Lime-juice, 1 lb. Preserved Meat, 6 oz. Suet, 8 oz. Raisins, 4 oz. Butter.

SUBSTITUTIONS at the following rates may, at the option of the Master of any Passenger Ship, be made in the above Dietary Scale—that is to say, 1 lb. of Preserved Meat for 1 lb. of Salt Pork or Beef; 1 lb. of Flour or of Bread or Biscuit, or ½ lb. of Beef or of Pork, for 1¼ lb. of Oatmeal, or 1 lb. of Rice, or 1 lb. of Peas; 1 lb. of Rice for 1¼ lb. of Oatmeal, or *vice versa*; ½ lb. of Preserved Potatoes for 1 lb. of Potatoes; 10 oz. of Currants for 8 oz. of Raisins; 3½ oz. of Cocoa or of Coffee, roasted and ground, for 2 oz. of Tea; ¾ lb. of Treacle for ½ lb. of Sugar; 1 gill of Mixed Pickles for 1 gill of Vinegar.

N.B.—Mess Utensils and Bedding to be provided by the Passengers.

GIBBS, BRIGHT & CO.,
1, NORTH JOHN STREET, LIVERPOOL.

Deposit.........£ 19 - -
Balance.........£ 20. 7. 6 To be paid at Liverpool before Embarkation.
£ 39. 7. 6

Received Balance ... day of ... 1869

Per ...

Passengers to be on board, for Medical Inspection, on 11 Aug at 9 a.m. o'Clock.

NOTICES TO PASSENGERS.

1. If Passengers, through no default of their own, are not received on board on the Day named in their Contract Ticket, or fail to obtain a Passage in the Ship, they should apply to the Government Emigration Officer at the Port, who will assist them in obtaining redress under the Passengers Act.

2. Passengers should carefully keep this part of their Contract Ticket till after the end of the voyage. N.B.—This is exempt from Stamp Duty.

This 'ticket for two souls' is for Room 15 in the second class and was sold by Gibbs Bright, of Liverpool, in July 1859.

The demarcation lines between the classes was strict, and the captain would take an active part in ensuring that they were properly adhered to. The behaviour of the lower classes did not apparently always come up to scratch. During the voyage of the *Great Britain* in 1865, Captain Gray had to post stern warnings addressed to the steerage passengers who had been walking on promenades that were outside their territory: 'We do not dispute but that they are as good men as any on board, who occupy the first or second cabin', the editors generously allowed, 'yet surely on that account they cannot expect to walk where they please. Had they desired this freedom, why did they not pay for it?'

The other main problem was gambling, and again, it was up to the captain to put a stop to the practice: 'On Wednesday last, we were much gratified and satisfied at seeing our Captain down in the steerage actively and forcibly reprimanding several of the passengers, who were gambling with cards. We trust that the authoritative remarks of the Captain respecting cleanliness and open air exercise will be obeyed, as such is necessary in that department.' Some years later, one of the steerage passengers was confiding to his diary that he was well rid of a chap from Strahane, 'a great card player and swearer . . . He lost two pounds the night before last and he sat up all last night at them. It was awful foolish work.'

However, it was not only the steerage classes who elicited reprimands from the editors of the ship's newspaper; smokers were singled out for attention and implored to refrain from 'the disgusting habit of spitting on the deck', and even the intermediate let the side down on occasion by 'permitting the stuff that inebriates to get into their heads'—getting drunk.

The Captain must have had his hands full. Not only was he responsible for the ship and the crew; he had to keep all classes of passengers happy and reasonably orderly. The success of a voyage depended almost as much on his social skills as on his ability as a sailor. John Gray obviously excelled in both tasks: 'such a good name as he bears, I have never heard given to any other captain', wrote a *Great Britain Times* reporter. People would wait six months to travel on the *Great Britain* rather than accept an alternative.

The loss of Gray overboard in 1872 might have been expected to have a devastating effect on the fortunes of the ship. In fact, she was nearing her end as a passenger ship by that time, and his successor, Captain Chapman, captained her for only five voyages.

Two years before the end, the ship carried some unusual passengers: a party of nuns, bound for the colonies to set up a new mission there. The leader of the party, Mother Mary Paul Mulquin, wrote a delightfully detailed diary which gives us our last view of the *Great Britain* in the twilight of her career before being relegated to a mere cargo ship.

At first sight, the ship did not impress. The nuns were thoroughly drenched on the tug carrying them out to the *Great Britain*. Life on board ship, they decided, was not the glorious scene people said: 'For our part, only the thought of going for God's Glory, would reconcile us to undergo the trial.' Besides, the ship herself was smaller than they imagined: 'Someone reported it to be three miles in length—an erroneous account.'

But by the time they had settled in their cabins, admired the decorations of the saloon, enjoyed the piano playing in the ladies cabin and the pleasures of walking on deck before breakfast, the old ship had begun to work her magic. The ice was broken once the weather worsened, and the saloon became a bedlam of flying plates, glasses and nuns. They met new friends; an obliging gentleman gave them German lessons, the captain 'shows us particular attention'.

Yet 'we shall be glad enough', Mother Mary decided, 'to relinquish (this) grandeur for our quiet convent repose'. But the memories of the vessel must have remained—of 'the calm water with a shining bright moon', of the dancing, singing and playing of the harp on deck, 'and to look from the stern to the opposite end of the G.B. you would imagine it to be a great village— the moon and stars beaming so softly—there are 800 people on board, all in perfect order.'

RULES FOR PASSENGERS

MEALS & BED-TIME.

1. Every Passenger to rise at 7 a.m. unless otherwise permitted by the SURGEON.
2. Breakfast from 8 to 9 a.m., Dinner at 1 p.m., Supper at 6 p.m.
3. The Passengers to be in their beds at 10 p.m.

FIRES & LIGHTS.

4. Fires to be lighted by the Passenger's Cook at 7 a.m. & kept alight by him till 7 p.m. then to be extinguished, unless otherwise directed by the MASTER, or required for the use of the sick.
5. Three Safety Lamps to be lit at dusk; one to be kept burning all night in the main hatchway, the two others may be extinguished at 10 p.m.
6. No naked lights allowed at any time, or on any account.

CLEANING BERTHS etc.

7. The Passengers, when dressed to roll up their beds, to sweep the decks, (including the space under the bottom of the berths) & to throw the dirt overboard.
8. Breakfast not to commence till this is done.
9. The sweepers for the day to be taken in rotation from the males above 14, in the proportion of five for every one hundred passengers.
10. Duties of the sweepers to be to clean the Ladders, Hospital & Dining Rooms, to sweep after every meal, & to dryholystone and scrape them after breakfast.
11. But the occupant of each berth to see his own berth is well brushed out; and single women are to keep their own compartment clean.
12. The beds to be well shaken and aired on deck.
13. Mondays and Tuesdays are appointed as washing days, but no clothes are to be washed or dried between decks
14. The Coppers & Cooking Vessels to be cleaned every day.

VENTILATION.

15. The Scuttles & Stern Ports to be kept open (weather permitting) from 7 a.m. to 10 p.m. and the Hatches at all times.
19. On Sunday the Passengers to muster at 10 a.m. when they will be expected to appear in, clean and decent apparel. The day to be observed as religiously as circumstances will admit.

MISCELLANEOUS.

17. No Spirits or Gunpowder to be brought on board by any passenger. Any that may be discovered will be taken into custody of the Master till the expiration of the voyage.
18. No loose hay or straw allowed below.
19. All gambling, fighting, riotous behaviour or quarrelsome behaviour, swearing, & violent language to be at once put a stop to. Swords and other offensive weapons, as soon as the passengers embark, to be placed in the custody of the Master.
20. No sailors to remain on the passenger deck among the passengers except on duty.
21. No passenger to go to the Ship's Cookhouse without special permission from the Master, nor to remain in the forecastle among the sailors on any account.

BY ORDER OF THE MASTER.

(Based upon an abstract of the QUEEN'S ORDER in COUNCIL of the 6th. October. 1849 for preserving order and securing Cleanliness and Ventilation on board of "Passenger Ships" proceeding from the UNITED KINGDOM to any of HER MAJESTY'S Possessions abroad).

The tableware reproduced on these pages has survived the years, almost miraculously. It was used in the *Great Britain* in 1845 and was supplied by John Stonier, founder of Stonier & Company, of Liverpool and Southampton. The design incorporates the Royal Coat of Arms and also features rope entwined in intricate patterns.

89

Replicas of the decorative features of the ship soon fired the imagination of visitors as the restoration work progressed. The gilt swan (*above*) stretched its wings and curved its elegant neck over the windows at the stern. The figurehead and trailboards, forward (*top right*) were restored to their 1845 state (as described on page 10). Another major step on the programme was the installation (*right*) of the replica of the original screw propeller (*Restoration photographs by South West Picture Agency*).

90

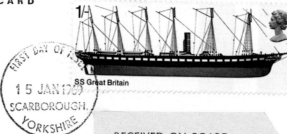

SS Great Britain

FIRST DAY OF ISSUE
15 JAN 1969
SCARBOROUGH.
YORKSHIRE

'GREAT BRITAIN'

RECEIVED ON BOARD
'GREAT BRITAIN'
AT
Sparrow Cove,
Falkland Islands.

Signed...................... 10 APR 1969

JOHN SMITH, Correspondent Member
s.s. Great Britain, Project Committee.

PHILART

"VOYAGE 47"
THE RETURN OF THE
"S.S. GREAT BRITAIN"
FROM THE FALKLAND ISLANDS
TO THE
GREAT WESTERN DOCK, BRISTOL

SS Great Britain

GREAT BRITAIN

23 JUN 1970

Built BRISTOL 1843

CARRIED ON BOARD
SS GREAT BRITAIN
FALKLAND ISLANDS
TO BRISTOL

"S.S. GREAT BRITAIN" LEAVING CUMBERLAND BASIN
ON HER MAIDEN VOYAGE 23RD JANUARY, 1845

OFFICIAL
"S.S. GREAT BRITAIN"
COMMEMORATIVE COVER

92

The authorities in both the Falkland Islands and the United Kingdom were quick to exploit the excited public interest in the return of the SS *Great Britain*. Two of the first day covers which recorded the journey and which are treasured by philatelists the world over are reproduced here. A handsome stamp featuring the vessel was later issued in Britain. Even today there is still keen interest among collectors in the project's outgoing correspondence which records the fact on each envelope that it was posted aboard the ship.

After all the worries and calculations about the *Great Britain*'s expected behaviour aboard the pontoon, the journey home was remarkably uneventful. The fact that the vessel had not been secured precisely along the middle line of the pontoon caused some concern at first; however, it soon became apparent that her odd diagonal position was not going to be a hazard.

These hitherto unpublished colour photographs show just how safely and securely the iron ship travelled across the Atlantic. A common reaction of seafarers who saw the bizarre convoy during the long ocean tow was how dignified the vessel appeared. Despite her 'stranded' situation, she still looked every inch a ship and not a hulk.

One of the earliest decisions taken by the SS *Great Britain* Project was that the ship should be restored to her 1845 appearance. This was not an easy decision to take, or a simple one, because it meant scrapping certain features of later designs which were themselves of historic value and general interest.

The photographs on this page and at left illustrate this policy in action. At left is a view of the stern after the removal of the 1857 stern frame. The replica of the original propeller was put aside for a time until the installation of the 1843 rudder post.

Laying the weather deck was an expensive and time consuming affair; during the second half of the 1970s it must often have seemed to visitors that there would always be temporary walkways. The view for sightseers shown above was not destined to disappear until almost the end of the decade, due to a combination of factors, including shortages from time to time of funds and labour, other priorities and the need to phase the decking in with the restoration of the gunwales and the elimination of various post-1845 features.

It was a slow task but the planking was put down with great care and professional skill in accordance with the Project's aim of restoring a vessel able to stay on show well into the twenty-first century.

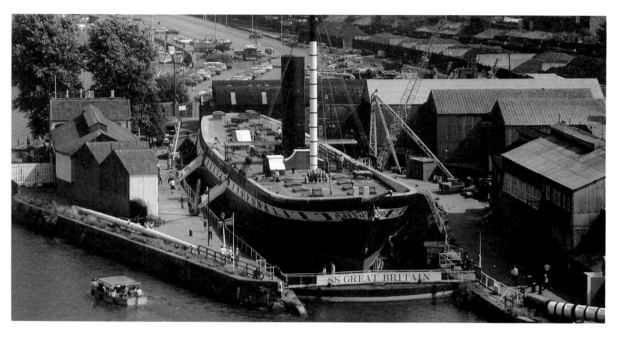

Nine years after the SS *Great Britain* had returned to the city, Bristolians and visitors were able to walk upon the planking of the weather deck. A year later there was the impressive sweep of deck, complete with skylights and companionway entrances, captured in these photographs.

The view (*left*) shows the decking forward, while that below makes it easy to appreciate how impressed the Victorians were by the spacious and uncluttered promenade towards the stern. Apart from the tremendous visual impact created by the completion of the weather decking, this operation has been of vital importance in keeping the ship weathertight and protecting the interior from exposure to the elements.

The vessel's appearance, as she entered her second decade in Bristol, had been further enhanced by the installation of a replica funnel, the main lower mast and the bridge, all donated by commercial firms. Below decks, three main bulkheads, the forward end of the boiler room, and the after part of the engine room had been fully restored. Away from the ship, work was well advanced on the construction of a full-scale replica of the original engine.

Bristolians viewing the *Great Britain* across the river from Hotwells in the early 1980s saw a vessel (*above*) which required only the 'days of the week' masts to make her indistinguishable from the proud creation of the 1840s. The dream of the SS *Great Britain* Project to restore the historic ship as a 'constant reminder of British enterprise, design and craftsmanship' was well on the way to becoming a spectacular reality.